Getting to Community:

Supporting people with developmental disabilities in their pursuit of the good life

Susan Stanfield

Spectrum Press

A DIVISION OF SPECTRUM SOCIETY

Spectrum Press, Vancouver, BC: 2012

ISBN 978-1-300-18380-8

The author gratefully acknowledges Michael Kendrick, John O'Brien, Barb Goode, David Pitonyak, Judith Snow and Lou Brown for their permission to reprint excerpts from selected publications.

Pictured on the front cover are Shauna and Barb. Barb lived in an institution from the time she was 10 years old through her mid-forties. When the institution closed, instead of moving into the community along with everyone else, she was sent to live in an extended care facility where it was assumed she would live out the rest of her days. But Barb had other plans. She wanted to live in her own apartment in the community. She was told this couldn't happen because she was too disabled. So she researched what services and supports were available and discovered that there were other people with significant disabilities living in the community, that it was possible. Then she was told by someone at the extended care facility that she'd need to learn how to read if she was ever to live independently. So Barb signed herself up for an adult basic education class at the local community college, headed off to school for the first time in her life, and learned to read. Finally, after 50 years of institutional living, Barb's dream came true. She moved into her own apartment with a roommate nearly 13 years ago, and hasn't looked back. Today, Barb spends her time doing advocacy work, public speaking, and writing her autobiography. She's looking forward to taking another college course. Barb has a large circle of family and friends she enjoys visiting with and is well known and respected in her community.

To my two co-directors, Ernie Baatz and Aaron Johannes

Table of Contents

Introduction

For the past 25 years, I have worked as a director of Spectrum Society for Community Living in Vancouver, an organization I co-founded with a group of friends in 1987. A few of us had worked for some of the more established service providers in the area prior to starting our own agency, in congregate programs that were typical of the services to people with developmental disabilities at that time. Some of the organizations we worked for had been started by families back in the 1950s and 60s, and their service models had been considered best practice at one time – the first community services for people who previously would have been kept at home and cared for by their families without any support, or sent to live in one of our province's three institutions. Some of these same parents had fought the government and local school boards for their children's right to attend school, a grassroots advocacy effort that led to British Columbia becoming the first province in Canada to provide publicly funded education for children with developmental disabilities. (Collier, 1995)

Fast forward to 1987, and the next wave of historic changes was unfolding, with the return of hundreds of people from our provincial institutions to communities across B.C. The institutional downsizing projects were the culmination of many years of advocacy, collaboration with all levels of government, and community initiatives led by local parent-run organizations and their provincial counterpart. In the 1970s, these organizations brought internationally renowned experts like Dr. Wolf Wolfensberger and Dr. John McKnight to our province, to consult with them on best practices and to inform policy and practice guidelines for the expanding human service sector. Both Dr. Wolfensberger and Dr. McKnight started up pilot projects in B.C. that advanced our province's growing reputation as a model for the rest of North America:

> "Our eyes and hearts were opened further when Dr. Wolf Wolfensberger challenged us with his Principles of Normalization, Citizen Advocacy Program, and Program Analysis of Service Systems (PASS). As a Visiting Fellow at NIMR [the National Institute on Mental Retardation in Ottawa] he was available to all Provincial Associations for training. [BCACL] invited his expertise and concurred with our national organization, CAMR, which chose the Principles of Normalization, the development of Comprehensive Community

Based Services (ComServ) delivery systems and integration into society as their goals for the seventies.

"The first Citizen Advocacy Program was begun in B.C. as a pilot project in Victoria under the Greater Victoria Association for the Retarded, with staff trained by Dr. Wolfensberger. Before the decade was out ComServ was going full swing in two areas of the Province – Burnaby and the East and West Kootenay Region 5. Training requirements geared up as a result of ComServ, which, to demonstrate alternatives to institutions and the value of integration, required the development of all needed services to be where the individual and family lived and to be a part of the services for all members of the community whenever possible." (Collier, 1995)

Wolfensberger's principle of Normalization and McKnight's expertise in community building strongly influenced the process of deinstitutionalization that unfolded over the next two decades in this province. Some of the earlier group homes that were set up in the 1950s and 60s had housed 10 or more people, and were often situated on the outskirts of town or in rural areas. The trend by the 1980s was toward smaller homes, situated in typical residential neighbourhoods. The downsizing projects furthered this trend, limiting the number of people living in new group homes to four, and locating these homes in communities all over B.C. The Province encouraged the development of new service providers and a range of service options, so as not to over-burden existing providers, who in many cases were already stretched to meet the growing demand for services in their communities. The opportunity to be part of these historic changes was exhilarating. Spectrum entered the B.C. community living scene as the last and largest of the three institutions, Woodlands School in New Westminster, was beginning to be phased out.

Closing the institutions was the focus of the community living movement in B.C. throughout the 1980s and 90s. Between 1988 and 1993, our organization supported 23 people to move out of Woodlands into homes in Vancouver. We took the "smaller is better" idea a step further and purchased duplexes, so two people could share a smaller home instead of four people all living together. We felt this would make for a more intimate living arrangement and allow for more individualized attention for each person. All over the province, dozens of new group homes were opening, new day programs and other support services were being developed. The result was a system of community-based services that was considered to be among the best in North

America. In 1996, B.C. became the first province in Canada, and one of the first jurisdictions in North America, to close all of its institutions for people with developmental disabilities.

The excitement of those early years, however, was starting to wane as the decade came to a close. Funding for new services had dwindled by the early 2000s, leaving service providers with few options for serving new people but to expand existing programs. Where some agencies had started downsizing their large facility-based day programs, or opting to keep residential vacancies open until someone came along who would be a good match for the other residents, they were now being pressured to serve more people with less funding, to fill vacant beds with the next available person, and even add a fifth person to those four-bed group homes. Budget pressures and increased competition for funding forced many smaller agencies to amalgamate with bigger ones; others simply went out of business. Our own agency faced the threat of elimination in one of many rounds of government restructuring that was accompanied by a growing emphasis on efficiency and standardization. This kind of thinking was far removed from the language of community building that had ushered in this new chapter in the community living movement just a few years earlier. The spirit of innovation was being overshadowed by a new focus on regulatory compliance. The introduction of accreditation in particular prompted a shift toward increased bureaucratization in the name of quality assurance, where achieving a successful survey result suddenly became priority one. Where just a decade earlier the service system seemed to be leaning toward more diversity in support arrangements and a broader range of options for individuals and families, the focus increasingly was on aligning service offerings to match prescribed models defined by funders and accrediting bodies that required ever more sophisticated technical knowledge and expertise to understand and implement.

John O'Brien, one of the most respected leaders in our field, saw this trend unfolding nearly two decades ago and cautioned that so-called quality assurance efforts not be allowed to over-ride the common sense of ordinary people, or create unnecessary barriers to inclusion. He urged service providers to stay focused on building good lives for people, rather than building bigger systems:

> "Services to people with developmental disabilities face a crisis of accountability. Uncounted thousands of hours of professional time and dollars of scarce public resources pour into enforcement of and compliance with increasingly complex regulations.

Administrators and professional advocates join forces to assemble a truly comprehensive set of quality assurance mechanisms and activities. Debate about assuring quality and safety fills the pages of journals and swapping anecdotes about the absurd distractions imposed (and accepted) in the quest for compliance fills hours at professional meetings.

"Alongside these debates about the administrative activities of quality assurance, a quiet revolution in the lives of a small but growing number of people with developmental disabilities redefines the terms of accountability. People with developmental disabilities who get opportunities and necessary assistance to grow up in reasonably well supported families, to go to school alongside their non-disabled brothers and sisters, to work productively, and to be an active part of the civic life of their communities, and to live in their own homes undermine the current logic of service delivery and thus the foundations of current activities to assure safety and quality. In new roles in new settings, more and more people with developmental disabilities emerge as having the same desire to author their own lives as anyone else does. So, if the service system's function is to promote human development, policies and practices which assume that people with developmental disabilities are passive objects of professional work must change." (O'Brien & Lyle-O'Brien, 1994)

Quality services, as defined by external regulations, do not necessarily translate into quality lives for the people who use those services. As the person who oversees the quality assurance activities at Spectrum, I am well versed in the language of efficiency, and the literally thousands of standards we are required to demonstrate our compliance with. I write policies and design checklists and reports that our staff and managers use for keeping track of various details and gathering information in support of these requirements. It's easy to make rules and put systems in place that satisfy the bureaucracy. It's much harder to craft a bureaucracy that accomplishes what it needs to without intruding on people's lives. The key, we believe, is having a clear vision and sticking to it, getting clear on what we stand for and don't stand for, to paraphrase our friend and business consultant Michael Walsh, who has helped us think through some of these issues. If we can stay focused on supporting people to build good lives, and figure out the simplest, most reliable ways of documenting what we do, the evidence will speak for itself. But if we let the regulations dictate our practice, we'll never get to building good lives.

A new generation has grown up in the 15 years since the institutions closed, the first of this post-institutional era. The first generation of youth to have experienced inclusive education is coming into adult services now. They're not looking for standardized program models and cookie cutter approaches, they're looking for flexibility and creative support arrangements. Their vision of a good life is grounded in the same kinds of everyday experiences they see their siblings and peers pursuing – in what John O'Brien describes as the *Five Valued Experiences*:

Belonging in a diverse variety of relationships and memberships.

Being respected as whole persons whose history, capacities and future are worthy of attention and whose gifts engage them in valued social roles.

Sharing ordinary places and activities with other citizens, neighbors, classmates and co-workers. Living, working, learning, and playing confidently in ordinary community settings.

Contributing by discovering, developing, and giving their gifts and investing their capacities and energy in pursuits that make a positive difference to other people. There are gifts of being and gifts of doing: contributions can include interested presence as well as capable performance. Contributions may be freely exchanged or earn pay.

Choosing what they want in everyday situations in ways that reflect their highest purpose. Having the freedom, support, information, and assistance to make the same choices as others of a similar age and learning to make wiser choices over time. Being encouraged to use and strengthen voice regardless of mode of communication, clarify what really matters, make thoughtful decisions, and learn from experience. (O'Brien, 2011)

In monthly orientations with new staff at our agency, I meet people who are friends and siblings and peers of these young adults, people who have grown up in an inclusive world, who attended school alongside students with disabilities. They have friends and family members who have disabilities, and they speak of them with pride and admiration. Often it's a personal connection to someone with a disability that has led them to work in this field. They say things like *"I was so inspired by my cousin, who has cerebral palsy and runs her own business,"* or *"I knew a guy in high school who had autism – he was an amazing musician."* Their assumption is that their peers will be doing more or less the same things they're doing – going to college, getting jobs, moving out on their own – and it doesn't occur to them that it would be any other way. The language of efficiency and standardization doesn't resonate with this generation. What resonates for them is John O'Brien's language of belonging, respect, sharing of ordinary places, contribution, and choice. Of course, I still refer them to our policies and procedures and tell them about the reports and forms they'll need to familiarize themselves with, but much more than getting a handle on the paperwork and administrative requirements, what they need is a framework for thinking about how to help people build good lives in community. That's where this book comes in.

With this book I'll share some of our learning over the past quarter century and some thoughts on this question of what constitutes service quality. These are not new ideas, nor are they all my own. Much of my thinking has come out of years of conversations and collaboration with my two co-directors, Ernie Baatz and Aaron Johannes, and from ideas that were articulated more eloquently and with greater depth by the pioneers of our field than I can do justice to here. The foundations haven't changed, but the world around us has changed. Attitudes have changed. Individual rights and freedoms that didn't exist for people with developmental disabilities are now being recognized, for the first time in history. The expectations of people coming into services have changed, and will continue to change as more people claim their rightful place in community. We need to be prepared to respond in new ways, and embrace opportunities to do things differently. This might require a rethinking of some of our old assumptions about services, and about what really matters to people.

The next chapter of the community living movement is being written right now, by the people who are living it. Self advocates are claiming this movement as their own, emerging as leaders in their own right as never before. The skills needed to support their self-determination – to support people to author their own lives, in the words of John O'Brien – are different skills than the ones we've relied on in the past. This book is for the front line supporters who will walk with this generation into the future and work with them to navigate a path forward.

Susan Stanfield

Long before there was a human service system, there was community.

Community living is not a new idea. It's how people have organized themselves down through the ages, in households and neighbourhoods, villages and tribes, cities and towns. We humans are social creatures. Our identity as individuals is inextricably tied to our membership in community. Community living is our birthright. We don't make a conscious choice to be in community, it's just the way things are.

The word community is derived from the Latin *cum* (meaning *with,* or *together*) and *munis* (meaning *gifts*). Simply speaking, community is about people coming together to share their gifts. Who wouldn't want to be part of that!

When we think of community, we think of the places we share with the people we love. We think of home. We might also think of communities of choice, or communities of practice, such as a professional community, a religious community, the arts community, and so on. The advent of social media has further expanded the concept of community. Just ask anyone under the age of 30 about their experience of community and chances are, social networking will figure prominently in their response.

There are obvious benefits to community membership – a sense of belonging, identity, security – but there are also responsibilities, both to other individual members and to the community as a whole. There's an expectation of contribution, a collective concern for the wellbeing of the community, as we see when people come together to help each other rebuild after a natural disaster, or to console one another after a tragic event. Renowned community builder and author John McKnight defines community as "a social space where citizens turn to solve problems." (McKnight, 1995). It's about giving of ourselves when we are able – helping our family, our friends, our neighbours – and trusting that when we need help, they'll be there for us. It's a reciprocal arrangement.

Occasionally we hear of someone opting out of community in favour of a solitary life, but this is by no means the norm, and most of us wouldn't entertain such an option. More often, when people leave community it's because they're forced out. Being expelled from community for violating the rules or for some act of betrayal is the ultimate punishment by a community against one of its members. Our yearning to belong, to be included in community, is so strong and so fundamental to our sense of self, that to think of losing our standing in community would be devastating for most of us. *If I'm not part of the community, where do I belong?*

But for people with developmental disabilities, community living has not been the norm. Their presence in community has not always been welcome. Throughout history, people with developmental disabilities have been removed from community, not for violating the rules but simply because they were different. They've been incarcerated in institutions, relegated to the margins of society, hidden from view – and rarely with any objection or awareness even on the part of other community members. They've just been quietly sent away. It's been such a common and accepted practice that until very recently the question of allowing people with developmental disabilities back into community has sparked heated debate, and sometimes outright hostility. Neighbourhood resistance was a significant obstacle in the early days of the institutional downsizing projects, in B.C. and elsewhere.

The service system attempted to allay some of this resistance by investing in new programs and services designed specifically for people with developmental disabilities, focusing on physical integration as a first step toward community living. Social integration, it was assumed, would just naturally follow as communities came to accept people with developmental disabilities as their neighbours and fellow citizens. Over time, the separate, formal structures would start to open up, the gap between *us* and *them* would be lessened, as the informal structures we all depend on in community – the sense of reciprocity, the goodwill of our fellow community members – would just naturally be extended to include citizens with developmental disabilities. Ryan would get to know his neighbours, they'd offer him a ride if they saw him standing at the bus stop, and in return he'd pick up their mail for them when they went on holidays. It would all unfold naturally, over time, as it does for the rest of us.

That was the plan, anyway.

Welcome to service-land

The human service system expanded rapidly through the 1980s and 1990s, fuelled by the assumption that disability-specific services were the key to achieving a good life in community. Somewhere along the way, we came to believe that a good life for someone with a developmental disability meant having lots of services: a residential service, a day program, specialized transportation and recreation services. These services were meant to facilitate community integration, but in reality, they often had the opposite effect. Instead of being a bridge to community, they replaced it. Services that were intended to be temporary or transitional became permanent. People who had been promised community living when they left the institution had made it to the edges of community, but weren't taking that last big step into it.

Aaron Johannes'
illustration of
someone "boxed in"
by services

The service system came to be a kind of closed community unto itself – "service-land," John O'Brien called it. The expectation of voluntary, reciprocal relationships and shared contribution that have been the cornerstone of community life through the ages was replaced by an expectation of specialized services. People could come into adult services and spend the rest of their lives surrounded by people who were paid to be with them, in environments that were designed especially for them – and not just the people leaving the institutions, but young people who had grown up in community.

Ryan didn't get to know his neighbours, because Ryan only ever went out with the rest of the people from his group home, in a special van. There was never any need for the neighbours to offer Ryan a ride. The natural opportunities for extending a helping hand didn't come up. The reciprocal relationships we anticipated rarely materialized.

The promise of community living wasn't that everyone would have a program. It was that everyone would have a life in community. That's not to say people might not need services, or that it's wrong to have paid people in one's life. It's just that services should *augment* the typical experiences and opportunities that are available to everyone, not replace them. Paid supporters should *enhance* and *support* natural relationships like family, friends and neighbours, not supplant them. Communities need to see people with disabilities as individuals with gifts and contributions to offer, whose presence in everyday places is enriching for everyone, and not see them as an imposition, or a separate group needing to be cared for in separate places:

> "Every single person has capabilities, abilities and gifts. Living a good life depends on whether those capabilities can be used, abilities expressed and gifts given. If they are, the person will be valued, feel powerful and well-connected to the people around them. And the community around the person will be more powerful because of the contribution the person is making." (Kretzmann & McKnight, 1993)

Attitude is everything

In his book, Blink: The power of thinking without thinking, Malcolm Gladwell looks at the power of assumptions people form about each other, almost instantaneously, or in the blink of an eye so to speak. We size each other up, often on the basis of subtle biases and personal prejudices we might not even be aware of. Gladwell refers to this as the "Warren Harding effect," a reference to the 29th President of the United States, "[who] was, most historians agree, one of the worst presidents in American history." (Gladwell, 2005). According to

Gladwell, Harding's imposing physical appearance contributed to his rise through the political ranks. At 6 feet tall with a "distinguished" air about him, Harding *looked* presidential.

Gladwell goes on to describe how he polled about half the companies on the Fortune 500 list – the largest corporations in the United States – and discovered that 58% of the CEOs were over 6 feet tall, compared to 14.5 % of men in the general population:

> "Is this a deliberate prejudice? Of course not. No one ever says dismissively of a potential CEO candidate that he's too short. This is quite clearly [a] kind of unconscious bias.... Most of us, in ways that we are not entirely aware of, automatically associate leadership ability with imposing physical stature. We have a sense, in our minds, of what a leader is supposed to look like, and that stereotype is so powerful that when someone fits it, we simply become blind to other considerations." (Gladwell, 2005)

Viewing a man's height as being positively correlated to leadership potential might be seen as an example of positive evaluation, ie. ascribing positive value to the attribute of height (unless you happen to be a short man aspiring to the top job at a Fortune 500 company). Conversely, we might also attribute low value to other qualities, as in the "dumb blonde" stereotype, or viewing people who are overweight as lazy.

Society's attitude toward people with disabilities can have a profound effect on how they experience the world, and their place in it. Attitudes have changed radically over the past half century, in light of changes to human rights legislation and generally more enlightened views of diversity in various forms. However, throughout history, the overarching assumption has been that the presence of disability represents a fundamental flaw in the person, and that people with disabilities are therefore inherently inferior, or less valued, than people without disabilities. Like the unconscious bias that correlates a man's height with his leadership potential, the presumed inferiority of people with disabilities is generally not spoken aloud, but can be seen as underlying a whole range of negative attitudes that have been used to justify discriminatory practices that continue to this day.

In recent years, a different assumption has emerged, one that locates the issue of disability within society, not within the person. This view holds that disability is largely defined by the limits of the physical and social environments people find themselves in, and that changing the environment, not changing the person, should be our focus. The concept of universal design, or barrier-free environments that are accessible to all people (ie. curb cuts on sidewalks, elevators, lowered light switches) makes it possible for people with physical disabilities to function more independently, without the need of special adaptations beyond what is available to everyone else in the same environment. This, in turn, helps to reduce the negative stigma often associated with disability. Similarly, changing the social environment to be more welcoming and inclusive of all people can go a long way to minimizing differences between people with typical social and communication skills and those with perceived deficits in these areas. An example would be using plain language and graphics instead of highly technical language in publications, informational brochures, etc. This not only benefits people with developmental disabilities, it benefits anyone with low literacy, people who are learning English as a second language, etc.

Judith Snow, an internationally renowned author, speaker and advocate for inclusion, takes this view a step further, arguing that there is no such thing as disability; that the problem is one of perception. Snow, who has quadriplegia and lived in an institution in Ontario before becoming the first person in Canada to get individualized funding so she could live on her own, rejects the disability label imposed on some by the so-called able-bodied majority, and instead focuses on the contributions that all people bring to community:

"Why are we called 'dis-abled'? We have different and unique characteristics. Often we are silent, or nearly so. Our bodies are unusually shaped. We are often fragile and frail. We live in intimate connection with other people's bodies, minds and hearts. Our ways are not inferior to others' ways. Living in this way challenges and extends our courage, our love, our empathy for others and our creativity. We see and hear what others miss entirely.

"I am not suggesting that everyone should be like us. Our gifts are rare, and that is good. But, as difficult as our bodies and minds can be, their very uniqueness brings strength and positive challenge both to we who live in these bodies and minds, and to society – when we are appreciated, respected and celebrated." (Snow, 2001)

The thing about assumptions is, they can become self-fulfilling prophesies. Someone who is assumed by others to be capable of learning will likely be provided with opportunities to learn, experience success, build his self-confidence, and over time will bear out the expectations that others have placed on him. Conversely, someone who is assumed to be incapable of learning will not be afforded such opportunities, will experience limited personal growth and development, and over time may come to see himself as incompetent, in turn reinforcing the assumptions others have of him. It's a vicious cycle.

Just as some people might have discriminatory or sexist attitudes toward women, or racist attitudes toward people of different cultures or ethnicities, others have pre-conceived notions about people with disabilities – disablist attitudes – that can be every bit as damaging. In fact, many people with disabilities would say that negative attitudes, assumptions and stereotypes are the biggest barrier they face, and not just from society at large but from those working in the human service system. As supporters, our own attitudes and assumptions about people's capacity can either help or hinder their personal growth and development, and can strongly influence how they are viewed by others. And so spending some time reflecting on our own attitudes and assumptions, individually or as a group in team meetings would be time well spent.

The tables below describe some of the common attitudes (negative and positive) toward people with developmental disabilities, and ways these attitudes sometimes get manifested.

Negative view of the person as...	Possible actions or manifestations
Less than a whole human being / lacking basic human needs or sensation	- lack of access to appropriate medical / dental care - inattention to physical comfort, eg. ignoring minor ailments (*"she has a high threshold for pain"* or *"she's not bothered by the cold"*)
Lacking capacity / incompetent	- describing people in terms of mental age (*"he has the mind of a two year old"*) - not being given choices or expected to assume responsibilities - low or no expectations for learning / acquiring new skills
Part of a homogeneous group	- referring to *"the blind"* as a group, or *"the handicapped"* - grouping people on the basis of disability or a shared diagnosis - promoting stereotypes / perceived shortcomings based on diagnosis, (*"he's autistic – they don't make friends"*)
Flawed / sick, diseased	- therapy / rehabilitation focus - prescribed meal plans, medication regimens, even if the person has no health related concerns
A burden on the family / source of shame or embarrassment	- viewing a child with a disability as a curse / punishment for sins of the parents - exclusion from family functions, eg. weddings, funerals
Pitiful / pathetic	- language of passivity / affliction, eg. *"confined to a wheelchair,"* *"suffers from cerebral palsy"* - charity focus, eg. telethons that portray people as helpless / victims
A social menace / deviant	- confinement in institutions or segregated programs - viewing sexual activity / expression of one's sexual identity as shameful or deviant, eg. sterilizations, labeling people as *"sexually inappropriate"* or *"promiscuous"* - justifying restrictive practices / punishment as a valid response to non-compliance (*"he brought it on himself"*)
Child-like / eternal child	- age-inappropriate language, imagery, activities – eg. referring to adults as boys and girls instead of men and women - over-protection / discouraging risk-taking

Positive view of the person as...	Possible actions or manifestations
An equal / whole human being	- access to needed health care and professional supports - attention to physical comfort, eg. dressing appropriately for the weather, tending to minor ailments
Capable / competent	- setting high expectations - opportunities for learning / acquiring new skills
A unique individual	- focus on positive attributes, eg. *"Sue loves dancing"* - spending time with people who share one's interests, rather than groupings based on shared diagnoses - positive images, media portrayals
As strong / healthy	- normative language, eg. *"exercising"* as opposed to *"therapy"* - normative approaches to meeting the person's care needs, augmented by specialized support only as required
A blessing to the family / someone with strengths and gifts to share	- having dreams, goals, aspirations / a vision of a good life - contributing to the family or household, eg. helping to care for aging parents, grandparents or young children - seeing the person's presence as enriching *("he's taught us to slow down and appreciate life more fully")*
Independent / self-determining	- active / empowering language, eg. *"uses a wheelchair"* instead of *"wheelchair-bound"* - finding role models, or being a role model to others, eg. through mentoring, advocacy
A contributor to society	- valued presence in neighbourhoods, schools, workplaces, eg. being part of the neighbourhood watch / block watch - learning about rights and responsibilities - having a job
Viewing adults as adults	- age-appropriate language, imagery, activities - viewing sexual activity / expression of one's sexual identity as normal and healthy - supporting dignity of risk / reasonable risk-taking

Implications for practice: from exclusion to belonging

Attitudes toward people with developmental disabilities have implications for how they get treated by others and by society as a whole. Viewing people as a burden or menace makes it acceptable, in the minds of those who hold this view, to marginalize or exclude them from the mainstream of community life. It's easier to justify sending people away if we believe they pose some sort of a threat. On the other hand, viewing people as equal citizens with contributions to make and gifts to share will lead to more accepting and inclusive practices. Just as there is a wide range of different attitudes, so there is also a range or continuum of possible responses that have shaped government policy and the evolution of the human service system, all of which are still evident today in one form or another.

Exclusion

At one end of the continuum of responses is exclusion, where the person with a disability is excluded or removed from community. The most obvious example of this response translated into practice is institutions, but even in the community people with disabilities can be excluded from things that other people take for granted, things like access to appropriate housing, health care or employment.

Segregation

Segregation refers to keeping people "with their own kind." Day activity centres are an example of segregated programs that are still prevalent today. Someone can be physically present in community but have little or no contact with ordinary citizens because they are kept segregated with groups of people who have the same disability label as they do, even if they share little else in common.

Integration

The idea of integration comes out of the civil rights movement, and it is speaks to the right of all people to have equal access to the same kinds of services and supports that everyone else in society enjoys. Integration was the guiding principle in the early days of special education and the adult service system. It focused on people with disabilities asserting their equality rights and gaining access to places and opportunities they had previously been excluded from.

Inclusion

Integration gave rise to inclusion during the 1990s. Inclusion takes the idea of integration a step further, and expects that people not only have access to the same opportunities and environments as everyone else, but that barriers in those environments be minimized or removed so that people with disabilities can participate fully. Integration put the responsibility on the person with a disability to "fit in," where inclusion puts the onus on community to adapt and make accommodations so that all people can participate fully. Where integration was about physical presence, inclusion is about meaningful engagement.

Belonging

Inclusion still carries an overtone of power dynamics – certainly meaningful engagement is better than mere presence, but even better than feeling that you are included is feeling that you belong. One can be included but not valued. Belonging denotes valued membership.

An example that illustrates the difference between inclusion and belonging can be seen in the way deaf people were treated in a small community on the east coast of the United States. For about 200 years on the island of Martha's Vineyard in Massachusetts, from the early 1700s through the end of the 19th century, everyone used sign language. One of the original families who settled on the island carried a strong hereditary gene for deafness, and over time the prevalence of deafness on the island grew to about ten times that of the mainland population. In her book, Everyone Here Spoke Sign Language, historian Nora Groce describes a community where hearing and deaf people communicated freely with each other, socialized, raised their families, and contributed equally in all aspects of community life. Deaf people weren't expected to adapt to the expectations of the hearing population, but rather, the community adapted to include all of its members:

> "Deafness was seen as something that just "sometimes happened;" anyone could have a deaf child. The Vineyarders' social response to this was a simple acceptance of the inability to hear.... They were truly puzzled by an outsider's interest in the subject. Almost all [of the people interviewed] believed that every small town in New England probably had a similar number of deaf people and adapted to them in much the same way. Many were genuinely

surprised when I told them that the incidence of deafness on the Island was unusually high."
(Groce, 1985)

Deaf people weren't considered to have a condition that required special accommodation; rather, deafness was simply seen as one aspect of diversity within the community. Just as some people were old and others were young, or some could run while others moved more slowly, some people could hear and others could not. And they all *belonged*.

The evolution of services

Large, government-run institutions were the predominant service model for people with developmental disabilities across North America, from the late nineteenth century through the 1960s. Institutions were seen to be in the best interest of both the person with a disability and of the community. Doctors routinely advised parents to institutionalize children with disabilities, to put them in the care of professionals. There were few services available in the community, and so keeping a child at home meant you were on your own. Many families simply couldn't cope or were made to believe they couldn't cope by professionals who convinced them that keeping their child at home would be detrimental to the child and to the rest of the family. It was not uncommon for someone with a developmental disability to live out his or her entire life behind the walls of an institution. The steady increase in institutional admissions through the first half of the twentieth century led to serious overcrowding. Coupled with chronic underfunding, institutions became little more than human warehouses. The institutional model went largely unchanged, and unchallenged, for nearly a hundred years.

Of course, not all parents listened to the professionals. Some kept their children at home and raised them on their own, without any support. During the 1950s, small groups of parents started to come together to explore other options for their sons and daughters, determined to give their children a chance at a normal life. Parent groups sprung up all over North America, as more people started to question the status quo. Education was an early focus for these families, with parents calling on school boards to provide some sort of program for their children with special needs. From there, they went on to advocate for other services like sheltered workshops and group homes, so their adult sons and daughters would have something to do during the day and options for places to live, other than institutions.

As community-based services expanded, more parents opted to keep their children at home, and institutional admissions started to decline for the first time in nearly a century. However, the shift from institutional to community models didn't happen overnight. Institutions had so thoroughly separated people from community that ordinary citizens knew very little about people with developmental disabilities, and had no idea what went on behind the walls of the institutions. "Out of sight, out of mind" was society's attitude. Unlike the very public protests of the civil rights movement and the women's movement, the community living movement developed largely outside of the public view, driven for the most part by families. People with developmental disabilities were not themselves in a position to organize and speak out about injustices, nor were they seen as capable of doing so. And so the institutional model persisted, much as it had for decades, even as community alternatives started to develop. It would be many years before people with developmental disabilities gained the same rights that other citizens took for granted, and started to make their way back into community.

In 1969, in the wake of a number of high profile exposés of the conditions in state institutions, and mounting pressure from families and advocacy groups for community alternatives, the President's Panel on Mental Retardation in the United States commissioned a report to look at models from around the world and recommend actions that would begin to address the problem of overcrowding and sub-standard conditions in America's institutions. Changing Patterns in Residential Services for the Mentally Retarded was a landmark document that brought together the leading minds in mental retardation research and practice from the United States, Canada and abroad. One of these leaders was Bengt Nirje, Director of the Swedish Association for Persons with Mental Retardation, whose submission to the Report introduced North Americans to the principle of Normalization.

Normalization

The idea of Normalization originated in Scandinavia in the years following the Second World War. Initially it referred to people with disabilities having access to social programs like universal health care that were being adopted in Norway, Sweden and Denmark, out of a concern for equality and human rights. Nils Bank-Mikkelsen, head of the Danish Mental Retardation Service, used the term Normalization to describe an overarching belief that "whatever services and facilities are open to all other citizens must, in principle, also be available to the mentally retarded." (Bank-Mikkelsen, 1969). Bengt Nirje expanded on this idea and formulated the first definition of Normalization, which he described as "making available to the mentally retarded patterns and conditions of everyday life which are as close as possible to the norms and patterns of the mainstream of society." (Nirje, 1969(1))

As in Canada and the United States, Scandinavian countries had institutions, but they also had a much more developed system of community supports and services that made it possible for parents to keep children with developmental disabilities at home and be assisted with child care, respite and educational services that were not introduced until much later in North America. Scandinavian institutions were smaller than North American institutions, and they were just one of several residential options that also included hostels and boarding homes, all of which were known to provide a high standard of care. Scandinavian social policies reflected generally more enlightened attitudes toward people with disabilities and a commitment to seeing all people enjoy a good quality of life, including those living in institutions. In his submission to the Changing Patterns Report, Bank-Mikkelson describes a typical institution in Denmark, where residents slept in rooms with no more than three people, enjoyed meals in a family style dining room, worked during the day and had access to various activities during their leisure time (Bank-Mikkelsen, 1969). By contrast, Bengt Nirje painted a very different picture of institutions in the United States. Nirje, who had witnessed the Nazi invasion of Europe and later worked at a Red Cross refugee camp, visited several institutions in the United States during the 1960s, and had this to say about what he observed:

> "In the last two years I have visited a number of public institutions in several states, and on each occasion I have reacted with disbelief and bewilderment to what I saw. I found it difficult to understand how a society which is built on such noble principles, and which has the resources to make these principles a reality, can and will tolerate the dehumanization of a large number of its citizens in a fashion somewhat remindful of Nazi concentration camps." (Nirje, 1969(2))

Nirje, along with many of the other contributors to the Changing Patterns Report, called for institutional reforms in America, based on the Scandinavian model of residential services. In fact, several states had already begun building new, smaller institutions as a way to alleviate over-crowding in large state institutions that had long since surpassed their intended capacity. The widely held view of the medical establishment of the day, which was supported by the

<u>Changing Patterns</u> Report, was that improving conditions in state institutions and building a network of smaller, locally administered facilities, was the optimal course of action.

American academic Wolf Wolfensberger saw things differently. Where Nirje and others advocated better institutional care, Wolfensberger opposed the idea of improving a system which he believed to be fundamentally flawed. Instead, he called for a wholesale dismantling of the institutional system:

> "I submit that the problem of residential services cannot be solved by working on a number of specifics at a time, or by calling for simple-minded, low-level measures such as more money.... We need a model of services that is appropriate to knowledge, resources and needs of the 1970s and beyond, and that is based on a contemporary perception of the nature and role of the retarded person in our society." (Wolfensberger, 1969)

Institutions were incompatible with Wolfensberger's concept of Normalization. His was a radical position, one that most of his contemporaries dismissed out of hand. But as the years passed, his insights proved to be spot on. In a later essay, Wolfensberger recalls:

> "Even among reformers in mental retardation, the "better institution" concept remained prominent until Normalization afforded an alternative vision.... [The] answers from even the most enlightened people to "what is the wildest reform idea you can think of" would generally have been – and at best – (a) rightful funding for segregated special education, and (b) more money for more smaller better institutions, more equitably distributed across one's respective state. And these are exactly the two directions into which post-World War II reform had been moving." (Wolfensberger, 1999)

In 1972, Wolfensberger proposed a revised definition of the principle of Normalization, which built on the Scandinavian idea of providing people with developmental disabilities equal access to the normal patterns and conditions of daily life. Wolfensberger's definition emphasized "the utilization of means that are culturally normative in order to establish and/or maintain personal behaviors and characteristics that are culturally normative." (Wolfensberger, 1972). Where the Scandinavian concept of Normalization focused on equal access to services and life experiences for people with developmental disabilities, Wolfensberger's Normalization applied to all socially devalued groups, and emphasized using normative ways and means to address people's needs rather than separate, specialist approaches. The prevailing view at that time was that people with developmental disabilities were incapable of learning, and therefore needed protective or custodial care. Wolfensberger argued that all people should be presumed capable of learning, and be provided with opportunities to develop their potential. Again, such ideas were unheard of at the time. In fact, the adult service system, which had been expanding for nearly two decades by then, was premised on many of the same fundamental assumptions about people with developmental disabilities that the institutions had been built on.

In many ways, the smaller institution idea had guided the development of community-based services, with people continuing to be congregated according to their disability-related needs and perceived level of functioning, and segregated in special facilities. Even in the school system, well into the 1980s, it was only children with mild mental retardation who were deemed to be capable of learning, and even they were most often kept in separate buildings or self-contained classrooms, apart from the regular student population, engaged in activity that bore little resemblance to the education their same-age peers experienced. Wolfensberger's principle of Normalization challenged these assumptions and practices, and had huge implications for both the field of special education and the rapidly expanding system of adult services.

Social role valorization

In 1983, Wolfensberger further refined the principle of Normalization, shifting the focus to the impact of social devaluation on groups of people considered to be less valued than the majority in society. Wolfensberger observed that throughout history and in every society, some characteristics or attributes have been considered to be more highly valued than others – for example, in modern North American society, attributes like wealth, high intelligence and physical strength are highly valued, while poverty, low intelligence and physical weakness or limitations are less valued. The more highly valued a person's attributes or life circumstances, the more positively he will be viewed by society, and the more likely he is to occupy roles that are valued by the society and to achieve a good life as defined by that society. By contrast, someone with attributes that are negatively valued will be more negatively viewed by society, will tend to occupy roles that are less valued, and will be less likely to achieve the good things in life. The challenge, then, becomes one of levelling the playing field so all people have the opportunity to occupy valued roles and overcome the potentially damaging effects of social devaluation. Wolfensberger adopted the term Social Role Valorization to replace Normalization, and defined it as "the enablement, establishment, enhancement, maintenance and/or defence of valued social roles for people, particularly for those at value risk, by using as much as possible culturally valued means" (Wolfensberber, 1983). He refined this definition in 1999 to "the application of what science can tell us about the enablement, establishment, enhancement, maintenance and/or defence of valued social roles," (Thomas & Wolfensberger, 1999) emphasizing the empirical foundations of Social Role Valorization in social science.

Our social roles form the backdrop for how we interact with each other. When we meet someone new, we typically ask them about where they work, where they live, about their family. We want to know what roles they occupy, where they fit in. Each of us plays many different roles, in our families, our workplaces, our neighbourhoods and communities. Some examples are listed on the chart below. People with developmental disabilities might enjoy fewer social roles, and often their roles have low social value, for example, service recipient, client, program participant, person in care, or perpetual child. Social role valorization would encourage opportunities for them to assume more valued roles like the ones described below, in keeping with the kinds of roles other people of the same age or same culture would occupy.

Personal relationships	**Work**
- son / daughter - brother / sister - aunt / uncle - boyfriend / girlfriend - spouse - friend - companion	- employee - apprentice - supervisor / boss - entrepreneur / business owner - taxpayer - consultant / trainer - committee member
Home	**Community**
- homeowner / tenant - neighbour - strata member - host - caregiver - gardener / housekeeper / cook - block watch member	- constituent / voter - customer - student / teacher - volunteer - member of faith community - athlete / coach / team manager - artist / musician / patron of the arts

While the later definition of Social Role Valorization doesn't prescribe specific actions to be taken, we can see how it has a number of implications for those in support positions:

The *enablement* of valued social roles suggests that valued roles don't just appear out of nowhere, and they likely won't appear unless people have access to typical life experiences in typical environments. As supporters, we need to cultivate opportunities for people to explore and learn about different kinds of roles that might be available to them.

The *establishment* of valued social roles suggests that we can assist people to identify valued roles they would like to fill, to learn about role expectancies, and take the necessary steps toward assuming those roles. For example, Todd might enjoy going swimming at the local recreation centre with his support worker. Instead of the support worker purchasing the ticket while Todd stands off to the side, Todd could pay for his own ticket – thus establishing himself in the role of paying customer, as opposed to being merely a participant in the activity of swimming.

The *enhancement* of valued social roles refers to building on established roles and enhancing the person's reputation by taking on new roles. For example, if I go to a hockey game, my role is one of spectator (and people who know me well might say a less than enthusiastic one at that). My friend Stephen, however, is what you might call a super-fan, a diehard Canucks fan. He watches every game, owns several Canucks jerseys, and phones his friends to celebrate (or commiserate) after every game. Everyone who knows Stephen knows that he's a Canucks fan, so they introduce him to other Canucks fans, they buy him Canucks paraphernalia for his birthday, and they see him as an expert on all things hockey. His role as a hockey fan is multi-faceted and in many ways eclipses his role as a client in the human service system.

The *maintenance* of valued social roles suggests that we need to be proactive in helping people to sustain valued roles over time. In our swimming example, if Todd gets a new support worker who doesn't know he can pay for his own swimming ticket, and the support worker reverts to paying for him, then Todd loses some of his independence, and also loses the valued role he established as a paying customer in his own right.

The *defence* of valued social roles speaks to the role of supporters in promoting and defending the person's right to assume the same kinds of roles that anyone else in the same activity or environment might have. Let's say Todd becomes proficient at swimming laps and decides he wants join the swim club, but instead of being accepted into the swim club he gets referred to an adapted aquatics program for people with disabilities. It could be that Todd is the first person with a disability to ask to join the swim club, and perhaps the coaches have pre-conceived notions about Todd because of his disability. We can see this as an opportunity to educate them about inclusion and showcase Todd's capabilities, so they get to know him as an individual with a positive contribution to make as a potential member of the swim club.

Culturally valued analogue

An important feature of Social Role Valorization is the idea of the culturally valued analogue, which suggests that our services and supports be guided by the usual ways and means that ordinary people use to address their needs, rather than by specialist or disability-specific solutions. The service system has generally favoured approaches that emphasize the differences or less valued attributes of people with disabilities, rather than the similarities or more valued attributes they share with other citizens. Group homes are a common response to the housing needs of people with developmental disabilities, but they're not at all common for anyone else in our society. The culturally valued analogue or normative response to one's need for home would be living with one's family, sharing a home with a roommate, or having a home of one's own. Using the culturally valued analogue as a point of reference is one way we can apply the principle of Social Role Valorization to practice, at both the program level and in our day-to-day interactions with people we support. Instead of looking to the service system first, a good rule of thumb is to ask, *"What's the culturally valued analogue for addressing this issue or concern?"*

Those in support positions can help to reframe the way others view people with disabilities, by promoting more valued social roles and a more positive image of the person as a contributing member of society. The eyes of the community are on us. By demonstrating an attitude of respect, and showcasing the person's strengths and gifts, we set a powerful example and convey to others that this is a person of value.

Wolfensberger inspired a new generation of leaders to begin shifting the focus of human services from protective and exclusionary practices to more empowering and inclusive ones. Exceptional Parent magazine declared Wolfensberger's work on the principles of

Normalization and Social Role Valorization as one of the "seven wonders" of the disability field, alongside such historic advancements as the discovery of the polio vaccine, Braille, and the wheelchair (Carter-Hollingsworth & Apel, 2008). His 1972 book, The Principle of Normalization in Human Services, was selected by a panel of leading special educators as the most significant contribution to the field of mental retardation in 50 years (Heller et al., 1991).

Out of the institution and into community

The human service system is a relatively recent phenomenon, dating back about 60 years. During that time, services have evolved in response to changing attitudes and the expectations of people who use these services. This evolution can be summarized according to three distinct approaches, which are outlined below and described in more detail on the following pages.

	Custodial Approach	Developmental Approach	Citizenship Approach
View of people with disabilities	- Burden - Dependent	- Tolerated - Capable of learning	- Valued - Enriching to society
Response to people with disabilities	- Exclusion - Segregation	- Integration	- Inclusion - Belonging
Role expectancies of people with disabilities	- Patient - Resident	- Client - Program participant	- Citizen - Community member
Staff roles	- Care aide - Attendant	- Vocational / residential care worker	- Supporter - Facilitator
Planning focus	- System-centred	- Program-centred	- Person-centred
Service focus	- Specialized services - Focus on compliance	- Continuum of disability-related services - Focus on rehabilitation and training	- Typical (generic) services augmented by specialized services - Focus on self – determination and empowerment

Custodial approach

The custodial approach assumed that people with developmental disabilities needed protective care in environments that were designed to meet their special needs. The focus was on creating a safe, secure, and controlled environment (although, in reality, custodial arrangements often made people more vulnerable by separating them from natural relationships and typical safeguards – I'll talk more about this later). The most obvious example of the custodial model was institutions, but it's not just large residential institutions that fit this model. Smaller settings can also be custodial, for example a group home where staff take on a parental role, providing care and supervision to the residents but not necessarily encouraging their personal development or providing access to typical life experiences. Even a one-person home can be a custodial arrangement.

The early community-based services tended to replicate the custodial approach of the institutions. The focus was on creating smaller, more normalized environments in the community, but with no working models to go on besides the custodial approach, many of the same principles and practices carried over from the institution to the community. People were congregated in groups and assigned to program placements according to their perceived level of functioning (which, it was assumed, would not change). Professionals and program supervisors became their *custodians*, often assuming complete authority over people's lives.

Compliance and standardization are key features of the custodial approach. The only real expectation of people in a custodial service is that they comply with the conditions set by those in charge.

Developmental approach

Unlike the custodial approach, which viewed people as dependent, the developmental approach assumed that people with developmental disabilities could learn to function more independently. It was based on the belief that all people pass through the same developmental milestones, and therefore the task of educators and service providers was to help people achieve these milestones in the usual order, however long that might take. A continuum of services evolved, the purpose of which was to get people "ready" for community living.

The developmental, or *readiness*, approach emerged in the 1970s and focused on teaching people skills that would lead to increased independence. At one end of the continuum were pre-vocational centres, where people would learn to sort nuts and bolts as a pre-requisite to assembly line work in a sheltered workshop. This, in turn, would prepare them to be part of a work crew or enclave in an actual community setting, and so on up the line to eventual competitive employment. The developmental approach had people learning to identify coins as a step toward one day having their own bank account, or learning social skills in a group activity program so that someday they'd be ready to have friends.

The problem was, most people didn't move through the continuum. Skills acquired in one setting did not transfer to other settings, and in fact people often regressed or lost competencies over time as a result of the low expectations placed on them and a lack of real life application for the skills they were learning. Programs that were intended to be transitional became permanent placements, where learning objectives gave way to custodial pressures as people kept coming into services, but rarely left. Barb Goode, well known self advocate and author of The Goode Life, recalls how she was held back in the group home where she used to live, even after mastering all the steps supposedly needed for her to move on to greater independence:

> "Exactly one year after I moved into the group home, I wanted to move out. But I was told I had to wait six months. During that time I had to practice life skills targets that the staff set for me. I role-played cleaning the house. I was taken grocery shopping, but the staff still did the actual grocery shopping. I did make-believe budgeting which didn't help me at all when I eventually got my own place.

> "For the last six months or more at the group home they were trying to teach me to do all these things, but I rebelled. They get you all prepped up, but then you don't really do anything. You have to be able to write up a budget, you have to be able to clean, and you have to pass all these different tests. What about the average person? Excuse me for saying so, but you don't have to pass any tests to be allowed to move out on your own. You just move. You learn as you go along." (Goode, 2011)

The chart below illustrates the continuum of services, with the most restrictive environments at the bottom end of the continuum and least restrictive at the top end.

The continuum of services

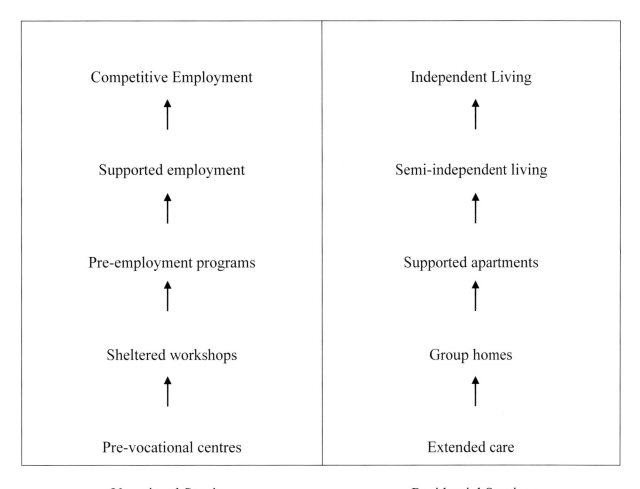

Competitive Employment

↑

Supported employment

↑

Pre-employment programs

↑

Sheltered workshops

↑

Pre-vocational centres

Independent Living

↑

Semi-independent living

↑

Supported apartments

↑

Group homes

↑

Extended care

Vocational Services   Residential Services

Citizenship approach

The developmental approach saw community living as something people would earn once they acquired the skills needed for independent living. The citizenship approach maintains that community living is a fundamental right of all people, not a privilege reserved for a select few. Rather than prescribing how people should live or what skills they should learn, the role of services, according to this approach, is to support people to take control of their own lives. The citizenship approach adopted many of the same principles, and even the language, of the civil rights movement. The custodial and developmental models were criticized for perpetuating *segregation*, where the citizenship approach advocated *integration*, and later, *inclusion*. Issues of *discrimination* and *equality rights* started being discussed in relation to people with developmental disabilities. The *community living movement* gained momentum as a kind of civil rights movement for people with developmental disabilities.

Political activism aimed at securing equal rights was an early focus of the citizenship approach. During the 1980s, some of the more progressive service providers began shifting their focus away from systems-driven custodial and developmental approaches to more personalized approaches that recognized people with developmental disabilities as individuals with unique strengths and interests, rather than viewing them as members of a homogeneous group. People with disabilities themselves started getting involved in boards and committees of organizations, forming peer support and self advocacy groups, where previously it had been parents leading the advocacy effort on behalf of their sons and daughters. An early focus for self advocates was pushing organizations to change their names from *associations for the mentally retarded* to *community living associations*, signaling a shift away from a charity perspective to one of empowerment.

Another feature of the citizenship approach that emerged in the 1980s was the notion of individualized funding. In Ontario, Judith Snow became the first person in Canada to obtain individualized funding, meaning she got the government to agree to carve off the portion of funds that were paying for her to live in an extended care facility, and have these funds given directly to her. Gaining control of her own funding allowed her to move into her own home, hire her own staff, and direct her own supports. In B.C., the Vela Microboard Association started in 1987 as a way to give individuals and families more control over their services, including, if the person so desired, securing individualized funding. A microboard is a small group of committed people who come together around one person with a disability and form a non-profit society (a *board*) for the sole purpose of supporting this one person. There are many other successful examples of individualized funding arrangements, in B.C. and across North America. However, individualized funding is still the exception, not the rule. Most of the funding for community supports continues to be directed to agencies for block-funded residential and day programs.

The 1980s saw many positive changes in the area of individual rights. The independent living movement, started by people with physical disabilities back in the 1960s, inspired people with developmental disabilities to start asserting their right to live independently. School boards were pressured into allowing children with disabilities to attend their neighbourhood school instead of being bused across town to segregated schools. Municipalities began enacting bylaws requiring buildings and public spaces to be accessible to people with disabilities.

These were monumental changes, all happening within the space of a few short years. It seemed as though the barriers were all coming down, and now it was just a matter of moving people back into the community to take up their rightful place alongside everyone else. Unfortunately, it wasn't to be quite that simple. Having equal rights brings with it an expectation of equal responsibilities: the right to make our own decisions is balanced by the responsibility for our decisions; the right to live in a home of our own brings with it the responsibility for maintaining a household, paying the bills, and so on. As time went on, people began to realize that while independence and equal rights are crucial, they represent a means to an end, and not the end itself. Integration doesn't guarantee belonging. Independence without relationships or valued social roles can make for a very lonely life. *Interdependence* more aptly describes what most of us strive for in our lives. We need other people, and we need to feel needed. Citizenship involves more than simply being present in community. It's about meaningful engagement, personal accountability, and reciprocity. These are some of the principles that are shaping the continuing evolution of services.

Legal rights

In the past, people with developmental disabilities were presumed to be incapable of understanding or exercising the same rights that other people took for granted. It was common for family members to be appointed as legal guardians, and in the absence of family the court might appoint the public trustee to manage the person's affairs and to give consent on behalf of the person regarding medical treatment, placement in residential facilities or institutions, and financial matters. Many of the people we supported to move out of the institution in the 1980s had legal guardians or were represented by the public trustee. None were involved in any of the planning meetings we attended, or had much say over where they would live or who they would live with when they left the institution. While in the institution, people had virtually no rights. They were confined to locked wards, had no privacy, and were not permitted to leave without permission. They could be medicated without their consent, denied medical treatment, secluded, and restrained. Chemical restraints (high doses of sedative and psychotropic medications) and the practice of pulling people's teeth instead of providing them with proper dental care were common practices in institutions. The sterilization of adults with developmental disabilities without their consent was permitted in our country up until the Supreme Court banned the practice in the landmark case of *Eve*, in 1987.

Canadian Charter of Rights and Freedoms

The Canadian Charter of Rights and Freedoms is a bill of rights for all Canadians, which outlines the rights and freedoms we are guaranteed under the law as citizens.

The first draft of the Canadian Charter of Rights and Freedoms made no reference to people with disabilities. It guaranteed equality before the law without discrimination on the basis of race, national or ethnic origin, colour, religion, age or sex – but said nothing about discrimination on the basis of disability. People with disabilities and advocacy groups protested, demanding that the non-discrimination clause be amended to include people with physical and developmental disabilities. Their advocacy was successful, and when the Charter was finally adopted in 1982, the non-discrimination clause had been revised to include people with disabilities.

"Every individual is equal before and under the law and has the right to the equal protection and equal benefit of the law without discrimination and, in particular, without discrimination based on race, national or ethnic origin, colour, religion, sex, age or mental or physical disability." (Canadian Charter of Rights and Freedoms, 1982)

The Canadian Charter of Rights and Freedoms is part of the Canadian Constitution, which is the highest law of the land. In addition to these over-arching laws, there are many other federal and provincial laws that deal with specific rights, for example employment standards, education, access to health care, and family law. Every law that gets passed in our country must respect people's Constitutional and Charter rights, ie. no other law, regulation or statute can override these fundamental equality rights that are guaranteed to all citizens.

United Nations Convention on the Rights of Persons with Disabilities

In 2010, Canada ratified the United Nations Convention on the rights of persons with disabilities. As a signatory to this Convention, Canada has pledged to respect and promote these rights. Some of the sections that are particularly relevant to the kinds of services we provide, and to the people we support are:

Article 12 – Equal recognition before the law: People with disabilities have the right to make their own decisions. Countries agree that they must take measures to provide people with disabilities access to the support they may require to exercise their legal capacity.

Article 19 – Full inclusion; independent living: People with disabilities have an equal right to live in the community, including where and with whom they live. It also means that people have access to disability-related services to support their inclusion in the community (and prevent their isolation or segregation from the community).

Article 27 – Employment: People with disabilities have a right to equal access to employment, which includes having access to work environments that are open, accessible, and inclusive. It also means having the assistance that may be required to find and maintain employment. (BCACL, 2010)

These are powerful statements that stand in stark contrast to the reality for so many who continue to live in places that others have chosen for them, and who are not employed or being supported to find employment. The full impact of the UN Convention remains to be seen; however, it provides a framework to guide our collective efforts going forward. It is a clear imperative for the service system to recognize and respect people's rights at a whole different level from what it's done up until now. The UN Convention is a call to raise the bar, to not become complacent or settle for selective recognition of people's rights as it suits our purposes. People have a right to expect that we listen to them, and that we provide them with the support they need to live good lives. They have a right to object when we try to fit them into pre-defined placements or impose a one-size-fits-all solution to their unique needs and life circumstances.

Today, people with developmental disabilities have all the same legal rights as any other citizen. However, having legal rights doesn't guarantee that those rights will always be respected. Those who support people with developmental disabilities aren't always aware of the legal status or rights of the people they support, so they might assume authority for decision-making rather than helping people make choices for themselves. Likewise, many people with developmental disabilities themselves need support in understanding and exercising their rights. While this poses some interesting challenges, a person's need for support is by no means reason for disregarding or minimizing his rights. Someone with a developmental disability might need help making some kinds of decisions, but be perfectly capable of making other decisions on his own. For example, John might be able to go to the doctor on his own and consent to changes in his medication, but need support to follow up on the doctor's instructions around monitoring possible side-effects, or determining when to go back for a follow-up visit. Our temptation in situations like this might be to take over, to go with John and speak to the doctor ourselves, on John's behalf. But in doing so, we convey to the doctor that John is not capable of speaking for himself. Another solution could be to ask the doctor to write down any instructions in addition to communicating them verbally to John, so John's supporters could sit down with him when he gets home and review the doctor's notes together. Or if John needs someone to accompany him to the appointment, John could still go in by himself to talk to the doctor in private and then call his support worker in when he's ready.

Supported decision-making

The assumption in the past was that people with developmental disabilities lacked the capacity to make informed decisions for themselves, ie. they were presumed to be incompetent. The legal definition of capacity was an all-or-nothing proposition: either you were capable of making all your own decisions, or someone else would make them for you. Supported decision-making strikes a middle ground between these two extremes. It recognizes that people might need support with some kinds of decisions, but not others, or they might need support for a period of time, but not forever. It presumes competence. Supported decision-making invites a more thoughtful and proactive approach to helping people lead their own lives to the greatest extent possible, with assistance from people of their choosing.

A few of the people we support have court-appointed substitute decision-makers (usually an immediate family member) who have the legal authority to speak for the person, or they have certain kinds of decisions made for them by the public trustee. Others have a more flexible arrangement, like a *Representation Agreement,* which is a legal planning document that allows a person to designate family or friends of their choosing to make specific kinds of decisions on their behalf. Representation Agreements originated in B.C., and were recognized in law through the B.C. Adult Guardianship Legislation – the first time anywhere in the world that the right of people with disabilities to have supported decision-making was recognized in law. Any person, regardless of their perceived level of independence, can have a Representation Agreement. In the past, the courts would often appoint a committee or legal guardian, without the person's consent, but with a Representation Agreement the person gets to choose who to designate as their representative.

It's important that staff know about and understand each person's legal status, including any substitute or supported decision-making arrangements that have been put in place, specifically:

- What is the scope of the person's autonomous or independent decision-making? What kinds of decisions does the person need support with, and who provides that support?

- If the person has a substitute decision-maker, what is the scope of that person's authority? Eg. medical consent, personal care decisions, financial decisions?

- What is the role of staff in helping people make decisions?

In the absence of clear guidelines or an agreed upon protocol for decision-making, staff often become de-facto decision-makers for the person, which raises a host of ethical issues and puts them in a potential conflict of interest. Unless people have a legal representative who speaks for them, or they've designated someone to help them with decision-making (for example, through a Representation Agreement), then they are deemed to have the same rights as anyone else, including the right to make their own decisions. They are presumed to be competent.

That said, everyone needs help making decisions from time to time. You and I consult with our family and friends, we seek professional advice for financial or legal issues, we talk to our doctor or get a second opinion for medical concerns. Families in particular have what Michael Kendrick refers to as a *natural authority* in the person's life (Kendrick, 1996), meaning that even without a legal agreement, families have an investment in the person's well-being and a long-term commitment that goes beyond the potentially limited involvement of paid services. In this sense, we should be mindful of seeing people within the context of their family first, and within the context of our services second, not the other way around. Sometimes our services start to encroach on parts of the person's life or even to assume responsibility for parts of the person's life that would normally be the domain of family, for example planning holidays or birthdays, looking for a new home, choosing a new doctor. It's quite common when someone enters the service system for staff to assume roles that family or friends might otherwise occupy. Families might even feel their presence is unwelcome, or that they should "let go" and let the service provider take care of things. Sometimes the message we convey when people come into services is that families aren't needed, that we've got everything covered. So instead of asking June's sister if she'd like to organize a birthday party for June, or help her sister pick out a new winter coat, the staff just do it themselves. In fact, inviting June's sister to help plan a birthday party or go shopping for winter clothes might be just the entry point she needs to become more engaged in her sister's life, or to maintain a connection. It might be just the kind of involvement that will help her to feel like she's a part of things, without being an imposition or feeling put upon to do more than she might be able to commit to. It gives her a role, and establishes a partnership that we can then build on. When it comes time for June's next planning meeting, her sister will be more comfortable offering suggestions and contributing to bigger decisions.

Alternative and augmentative communication

"The right to communicate is both a basic human right and the means by which all other rights are realized. All people communicate. In the name of fully realizing the guarantee of individual rights, we must ensure:

- That all people have a means of communication which allows their fullest participation in the wider world;

- That people can communicate using their chosen method; and

- That their communication is heeded by others.

"Where people lack an adequate communication system, they deserve to have others try with them to discover and secure an appropriate system. No person should have this right denied because he or she has been diagnosed as having a particular disability. Access to effective means of communication is a free speech issue."

(TASH Resolution on the Right to Communicate, 2000)

Decision-making goes hand in hand with communication. The ability to communicate – to express ourselves, be understood by others, and understand what others are saying to us – is something most of us take for granted. But for people with developmental disabilities, communication can be a major barrier to their independence and self-determination, especially if they don't use speech, or if their speech is very limited. If people are to contribute to and even lead their own planning and decision-making, a reliable communication system is a must.

The UN Convention acknowledges a wide range of modes of communication, beyond speech:

"'Communication' includes languages, display of text, Braille, tactile communication, large print, accessible multimedia as well as written, audio, plain-language, human-reader and augmentative and alternative modes, means and formats of communication, including accessible information and communication technology. 'Language' includes spoken and signed languages and other forms of non-spoken languages." (UN Convention, 2006)

We typically think of spoken language when we think of communication, but in fact much of our communication is non-verbal: our body language, tone of voice, and facial expressions often convey as much or more than our words. A common assumption is that if people aren't able to express themselves in conventional ways (with speech or sign language), they aren't communicating. In fact, everyone communicates. We might just need to pay closer attention to a person's non-verbal communication, and think creatively about ways to deepen and expand on other modes of communication like the ones mentioned above. We might need to listen more deeply. I'm reminded of Lara, who doesn't speak or use sign language, but expresses herself in other ways. She will position herself next to people she likes, or next to items she is interested in. She breaks out in a huge smile when she's happy, and when she's really happy she giggles. When she's bored, she'll start rocking back and forth, and if nothing happens to alleviate her boredom she'll start pacing the floor, or she'll grab hold of someone and pull them toward the door. She makes different vocalizations depending on her mood. Lara lived in an institution for the first forty years of her life, never went to school, and was described to us as having profound mental retardation. If you were to meet Lara for the first time, you might think she would be unable to communicate her wants and needs, but those who know her will tell you she's a great communicator. They'll tell you what Lara's different vocalizations mean. They'll explain how they observe Lara's body language, facial expressions and movements as cues to her mood and to determine her response to new situations or new people. They'll tell you how Lara chooses the activities she wants to take part in, what kinds of things she likes doing and doesn't like doing, who she likes spending time with and who she's not so fond of, what kinds of environments she's most comfortable in. Her daily and weekly schedule is comprised of activities of her choosing, which she takes part in with people of her choosing. She communicates all of this and more, without words.

Another false assumption would be to equate an inability to speak with a lack of understanding or comprehension. Sometimes people have limited *expressive* communication (ie., they have trouble expressing what they want to say), but very good *receptive* communication (ie., they understand more than people might give them credit for). We should always assume that people have the capacity for both expressive and receptive communication. The question, then, isn't whether people are communicating or not, but how we might listen better, and give people the tools they need to communicate most effectively.

There are many different kinds of alternative and augmentative communication strategies, ranging from the concrete to the more abstract. At one end of the continuum are concrete objects, starting with real-life items that are part of a given activity (for example, a fork representing mealtime) and representative objects (a miniature plastic fork). There are different ways to incorporate objects into a communication system, for example having a shelf or box with an assortment of objects that are used in different activities, or a portable system, like a backpack containing miniature representative objects that the person can use for making choices throughout the day, or to indicate a desire to initiate one activity or another. This kind of system is helpful for someone who has difficulty understanding more abstract representations, like photographs, symbols, or written words.

Pictures, images and written words are more abstract than objects. They can be used in a variety of ways – for example, daytimers, calendars, picture boards, or photo albums with pictures of the activities, people and places that are important to the person. There's also a wide assortment of technological communication systems, ranging from the low tech (laser pointers, simple switches) to high tech (computer voice generators, i-pads).

Whatever communication system is used, it's important that everyone supporting the person understands the system and uses it consistently. For someone who has never had a communication system, it might mean starting with a few concrete choices, and ascribing meaning to the person's gestures or behaviour as a way to *shape* new communication skills. For example, the team's consensus might be that when Jay stands near the front door, he's communicating that he wants to go out, so everyone agrees to respond to this action by saying *"oh, you want to go out for a walk, sure, let's go!"* Over time, Jay learns that his action (standing near the door) will result in a predictable response (going out).

Do no harm: David's story

The Hippocratic imperative to "do no harm" occurs to me often in this work. We're part of a system that, for all its progressive steps, has also done tremendous harm to people with disabilities and their families. It wasn't bad or evil people doing these things. It was people like you and me, people with ideas they believed to be right, and who acted, for the most part, out of good intentions.

Parents talk about the heart-wrenching decision to institutionalize their child, how it went against all their instincts, but how doctors and social workers convinced them it was for the best: "Forget about this baby, go home and have another one," was the advice of the professionals.

We can't understate the sacrifices these families made, only to be let down by the very system that promised to take care of their loved one. I recall a conversation with the mother of a 37-year old man with Down syndrome, David, who we supported to move out of the institution he had lived in since birth. In the spirit of re-engaging families, we had sent letters to the parents of the men and women who would be coming into our organization's services. In the letter, we said we'd follow up with a phone call, unless the family wished not to be contacted. I hadn't heard back from David's mother, so I phoned her and introduced myself.

"I'm with Spectrum Society, the organization that's setting up a home in the community for David," I began. After a brief silence, a quiet voice on the other end of the phone line replied, "David has been a living death to us." I'll never forget those words.

Her voice shaking, David's mother recounted how when he was born, the doctor had told her to leave him at the hospital, to go home and forget about him. She told me how she wanted more than anything to keep her son, but her husband said she'd have to choose between him and the baby. "I had no choice," she told me. Now, 37 years later, we were inviting her back into David's life – a life in the community, because the institution, it turned out, hadn't been such a good idea after all.

David's mother wasn't interested in the latest trends in human services. She didn't want to hear about all the wonderful opportunities that lay waiting for her son in his new life. Her heart was broken. And even if she'd wanted to reconnect with him, what was she supposed to do?

Walk back into his life after 37 years and pick up where they left off? She was a stranger to him.

Never mind that the damage of the past had been done before I was even born, to David's mother I was part of the same system that tore her family apart and never bothered to apologize or take responsibility for it. To David's mother, I was just another professional telling her what was best for her son.

And she was right. There were no guarantees about anything I was telling her. People like David had never lived in the community. Maybe things wouldn't work out for him. What if his mother took a chance and trusted the system once more, only to have her heart broken all over again?

She asked that I please not contact her again.

If we've learned anything from the past, it's that we don't have all the answers. These are people's lives we're talking about, people's brothers and sisters, sons and daughters, and their families are trusting in us to do right by them. We owe it to these families to proceed with humility, heed the lessons of the last half century, and do no further harm.

Building a good life is a journey, a process of exploration and discovery. Starting from the time we're very young, most of us are exposed to a variety of experiences, different people, places, activities and perspectives that give us a sense of what the world has to offer, what possibilities exist. We watch how other people go about their lives, and we learn from their example. We start to imagine what our future might look like. We start to dream. People ask us questions like "*what do you want to be when you grow up?*" and "*what's your favourite subject at school?*"– questions that reflect assumptions about our capacity as critical thinkers, as individuals with hopes and aspirations all our own. As we get older, we venture out into the world, meet new people, try out different jobs and different living arrangements. We begin to build our life.

People with developmental disabilities might not be exposed to the same opportunities for exploration and discovery. They might not get asked as children what their favourite subject is in school, or what they want to be when they grow up. They might not be taking the usual subjects that other children take in school. They might be perceived as being unemployable, even from a young age, and presumed to be destined for a lifetime of custodial care. Their network of friends might be limited to their peers with disabilities, or family friends. They might not get a part-time job in high school, or start dating, or get a driver's license – the kinds of things other teenagers do. The options available to them when they leave school are often very limited. While they experience the same life transitions as anyone else – finishing school, separating from their parents – instead of these milestones being a catalyst for personal growth and increased independence, often they highlight a widening gap between the reality of their daily life and that of their same-age peers. Where the rest of us are given the latitude to test our boundaries, people with developmental disabilities are sometimes held back in protective environments much longer, prevented from taking ordinary risks or charting their own path.

Quality of life

"There is a profound difference between having a life in community and flourishing as a human being." (Kendrick, 2009)

The question of what constitutes quality of life has been the subject of philosophical debate down through the ages. The answer might vary from one person to another or from one culture or community to another, but there are some common elements that most people would agree are important for a good life. There's been an assumption that there's a different set of criteria by which the quality of life of someone with a developmental disability is measured, a kind of modified quality of life that focuses on the person's physical and material needs – being safe, secure, and well cared for. A parent once told me that when people would ask what kind of a future she envisioned for her son, Peter, she would say, "I just want him to be happy," by which she meant she wanted him to be safe, secure, and well cared for. When people asked her what she envisioned for her other children, she would talk about them having friends, having homes of their own, jobs they enjoyed. It dawned on her one day that Peter, who happens to have cerebral palsy, might dream of having all these things too, and that by limiting her vision of what was possible she was holding him back. For many years, she had assumed he would eventually move into some kind of specialized facility, and that he would be in the care of specially trained people his whole life. Then she started dreaming bigger. Instead of assuming that Peter would never live on his own, she started imagining what would need to happen for him to have the kind of life she envisioned for her other children. What support would need to be put in place for him to have his own apartment, to have relationships of his choosing, to have a rich life in community?

Today, Peter lives in his own apartment in a co-op complex with an unpaid roommate, a college student he selected from a number of applicants who responded to his ad for someone to share his apartment. They're two guys living on their own for the first time, experiencing the same life transition in much the same way. They host parties. They hang out together. At Hallowe'en they decorate the common room of the complex and hand out candy to trick-or-treaters. Peter has a team of support workers he's chosen, who help him plan his day, pick up groceries for dinner, get to his music and fitness classes, visit with family and friends – the usual kinds of things that people his age like to do. Peter is safe, secure, well cared for...and he has a great life.

A while back, we hosted a day-long conversation with a group of people with disabilities and their supporters, to explore this question of what constitutes a good life. We wanted to check out our own assumptions about what *we* thought was important, and what the research tells us about what makes for a good quality of life. We were also interested to hear about any barriers people perceived as holding them back from getting the life they wanted. I've summarized the ideas that came out of this discussion below, starting with some thoughts on what makes for a good life, and then some of the things people saw as getting in the way of a good life:

What makes for a good life?

- Relationships / family, friends
- Health & well-being
- A sense of purpose
- Freedom, choice, opportunity
- Having enough money
- Taking risks
- A sense of belonging
- Love
- Home, a safe place of one's own
- Safety and security
- Being respected / listened to / valued
- Activities in community
- Understanding one's gifts and being able to share them

What gets in the way of having a good life?

- Being lonely or isolated
- Feeling a lack of control
- Too many rules / bureaucracy
- Learned helplessness
- Having others make decisions for me / about me
- Being ignored / disrespected
- Being over-protected / not allowed to take risks

- Not being taken seriously
- Poverty / not having enough money
- Having unmet needs
- Segregation
- Low self-esteem / self-confidence
- Lack of communication skills
- Prejudice / being viewed negatively by others

Not surprisingly, the things people identified as being important for a good life are the same things most anyone else wants. But when we look at the list of what gets in the way of a good life, we see some differences. Some of the barriers people identified are directly related to the human service system. In fact, much of the discussion with our focus group centred on the ways in which services sometimes get in the way of having a good life. There was a strong sense that people felt pressured to surrender some of their control and choices when they entered the service system. Some went so far as to say they had left services or refused support in the past because of how a service provider infringed on their autonomy. For example, a woman who was recovering from surgery had homemakers come in to assist with some of the heavy housekeeping tasks, and before she knew it the homemakers were organizing her personal belongings, taking charge of her meals, telling her she needed to go on a diet. "We need help with one part of our life, and people assume we need help with everything – we lose our independence," she said. This was a recurring theme in the discussion.

Who holds the power?

"People should not have to give up their rights as citizens in order to receive the supports they require to live good lives." (Lord, 2001)

Paternalism has been a driving force behind the human service system, stemming from the age-old view of people with developmental disabilities as lacking competence. Paternalism means acting on another person's behalf, or making decisions on behalf of the person, without the person's explicit consent.

Paternalism in our field gets expressed in a many different ways:

- A culture of *doing for* people rather than *working with* them;
- Restrictive policies and practices applied across-the-board – for example, keeping everyone's medications in a locked cupboard, even if some people are able to manage their own medication;
- Presuming incompetence rather than presuming competence – for example, transporting people in a house van or staff vehicles instead of teaching them to use transit;
- Giving staff control over aspects of the person's life or over decisions that belong with the person, for example taking control of the person's money;
- Not informing people about their rights or not supporting people to exercise their rights, eg. the right to choose their own doctor, the right to choose where they live;
- Offering people limited choices based on what others believe to be appropriate for them, eg. going bowling might be an option, but going to a night club is not;
- Withholding information from people "for their own good" – for example, not telling someone that a family member passed away, or not allowing them to attend the funeral, because it might be too upsetting;
- Making false promises, or failing to follow through on promises (*"we'll get ice-cream tomorrow..."*)

It can be challenging striking a balance between ensuring people's safety and supporting their right to make their own decisions. How do we respond when we see someone making unsafe choices, or refusing offers of help to deal with, say, an abusive relationship or an addiction? When does the duty of care that is vested in our role as supporters override the person's right to make his own choices? Getting back to the question of supported decision-making, these kinds of dilemmas highlight the need for clarity around who helps the person make decisions, and what the role of staff is in facilitating decision-making.

Some of the barriers to a good life that people identified point to a power imbalance, where service providers hold more of the power and the person receiving services has less power. In many of our traditional services, the agency holds the funding for the person's supports and sets the parameters for the service, such as hiring staff, deciding what hours staff will work, and the scope of their duties. The services available may not always align with what people require to live a good life. For example, Paul might need a place to live, but the only available housing option is a vacancy in the agency's group home, and so in order to satisfy his need for a home Paul must now live with three other people he hasn't chosen to live with, and adhere to licensing rules that dictate when he's allowed to be home, how his medications get handled, etc. Paul might be perfectly capable of spending periods of time on his own, but because licensing requires staff to be on-site whenever people are in the group home, he now has staff with him all the time – or he's not allowed to come home during the day if he feels like it, because the afternoon shift doesn't start until 3:00. The group home probably has rules regarding visitors, overnight guests, pets, alcohol, and any number of other issues that might further restrict Paul's lifestyle and choices. There might be one doctor or psychologist who everyone in the group home sees, and Paul will now be expected to see the same professionals as everyone else. The kinds of choices available to Paul might be very limited in scope, like choosing what to eat for breakfast or what colour to paint his bedroom. Think about the kinds of choices we make in our own lives, and how it would feel to surrender some or all of these choices to strangers, just so we could have a place to live, choices like:

- Where you live
- Who you live with / who you spend time with
- What you do in your spare time
- What kind of work you do / where you work
- What doctors you see
- What medications you take
- What personal information you share, and with whom
- How you spend your money
- What you eat and drink
- Who touches your body
- What self-care skills you learn
- What groups or clubs you belong to
- What faith community you worship with, if any
- How your home is furnished
- What time you go to bed / get up in the morning
- How you get around / your mode of transportation

Empowerment

"If we've learned one thing from the civil rights movement, it's that when others speak for you, you lose." (Ed Roberts, quoted in Driedger, 1989)

The conversation about empowerment and people with developmental disabilities is largely a conversation about how to re-empower people who have had their power taken away, or awakening a sense of empowerment in people who might never have believed they had any power in the first place – helping them find their voice, so to speak. We often meet people who don't know about their rights, who have never voted, never had their own bank account. They might be so accustomed to other people doing for them that they go along with whatever arrangements people might suggest because it doesn't occur to them to ask for something else. Unquestioning compliance should not be mistaken for informed consent. We have a duty to inform people about their rights and seek their input to decision-making, even if they're not asking to be consulted.

Another aspect of empowerment is the degree of control or influence individuals have over decision-making related to the structuring and delivery of their services. Michael Kendrick identifies 6 levels of empowerment regarding service design and decision-making (Kendrick, 2011):

Level 1   The person is passive / compliant; the system is in control and making all the decisions

Level 2   The person is selectively informed of decisions that are made by others on their behalf

Level 3   The person is selectively consulted about decisions that affect them (but not about all decisions and perhaps not about the most important ones)

Level 4   The person makes a significant minority of decisions for himself / herself

Level 5   The person makes a significant majority of decisions for himself / herself

Level 6   The person makes most of his / her own decisions

There's a wide range of service delivery models, or ways that a person's services might get organized and delivered, each premised on different assumptions about power and authority. At one end of the continuum are block-funded programs, where funding goes to an agency to provide services to groups of people, for example a group home or group-based day program.

At the other end of the continuum is individualized funding, where a person with a disability gets funds directly to pay for his own supports, with or without the assistance of a service provider. Typically in block funded programs, most if not all of the authority rests with the service provider, while with individualized funding the person (assisted by family or significant others) holds the authority for deciding what supports the person needs and how that support will be arranged. In between are various models for sharing the authority, for example *host agency agreements*, which are a three-part contract between the funder, the agency and the person or the person's representative. Our own organization's services are comprised of a combination of these arrangements. While the scope of each party's authority is spelled out more explicitly in a host agency agreement or an individualized funding arrangement, even in our more traditional services there are things we can do to personalize the arrangement and give people more of a say over decisions that affect them. Some examples of things we've done at Spectrum to shift the balance of power and give people more authority over decisions about the structure and delivery of their services are:

- Supporting people to move out of congregate housing into homes of their own, with roommates of their own choosing;

- Recruiting based on the identified qualities that each person has told us are most important to them in a supporter, as opposed to standardized criteria, for example *"I want to be supported by people my own age who share my passion for country music,"* or *"someone who loves being outdoors, has an active lifestyle, and has connections to people and groups in my community"*;

- Involving people in interviewing prospective new support workers, and giving people the final say over who gets hired into support roles;

- Providing people with information and resources to support informed decision-making, instead of making decisions for them – for example, teaching people about nutrition and planning their own meals instead of having an imposed menu plan;

- Creating individualized budgets, and sharing budget information with the person;

- Facilitating a variety of planning methods, and having people choose a format they're comfortable with, instead of having one prescribed approach to planning;

- Supporting people to deal directly with doctors and professional supports, eg. making their own appointments, having someone of their choosing accompany them;

- Creating time and space for personal relationships – for example, Brian is supported to have his girlfriend stay overnight on weekends;

- Involving people in team meetings with their supporters, or not meeting at all unless the person is present;

- Supporting people to manage their own personal funds and do their own banking;

- Using support hours flexibly – for example, Bev has a pool of hours available to her so she can schedule staff of her choosing when she needs them, rather than having a pre-set schedule of shifts;

- Enlisting natural supports – for example, Shaun, who doesn't speak, likes going to his neighbourhood coffee shop on his own. When he's ready to leave, he gets the staff at the coffee shop to call his support worker and they arrange where to meet;

- Involving people in training new support workers, including sharing information about themselves in the first person rather than the manager talking about them in the third person.

Shifting from an agency-directed to a more person-directed approach has been a focus in our organization for the past few years. We came to realize that while some individuals were very much in control of their own lives, others were not, and in fact sometimes the opposite was happening – sometimes people surrendered a great deal of control to the anonymous authority of "the system." Without meaning to, our services sometimes perpetuated old paternalistic assumptions and practices. And so we've been working to ensure that everyone has a say over how their supports are arranged, even those in our more traditional services. My colleague Ray Hunter cautions that it can take time for people to get used to the idea of empowerment, and to trust that changing the way we talk about providing support isn't just so much rhetoric:

"Our message to [people] might be "tell us what you want and how we can help" but it may take a while for that message to be trusted; and we have to prove to people that we will do what we say we will do. We support the self-direction by understanding that it may need time. Time for the individual to find their voice, find their direction. Time to prove that we won't just step in and take over if they are uncertain."

Self determination

Self determination flows from empowerment. It is based on the idea that everyone can lead his or her own life, with appropriate support. Self determination is a philosophy that has been embraced by human rights groups worldwide, including people with physical disabilities, and more recently by people with developmental disabilities. It stands in direct opposition to the notion of paternalism.

Self determination can be viewed in many different ways. In the school system, it's sometimes used as a framework for students taking an active role in setting their own learning goals and planning for what they want to do when they leave school. In adult services, it's a guiding principle for individuals and families who want to direct their own supports, for example through individualized funding or a host agency agreement.

The Center for Self Determination (www.centerforself-determination.com) defines self determination according to four key elements:

1.   *Freedom*

People must have the freedom to make fundamental life choices – where and with whom to live, where to work, how to spend their time;

2.   *Authority*

People must have real authority over their lives. This includes having control over the supports and services they receive;

3.   *Support*

People must have support to understand the options available to them, support to access opportunities for personal growth and development, and support to make informed choices;

4.   *Responsibility*

Individual rights are balanced with responsibilities. As people gain control over their lives, they will be able to assume greater responsibility for their choices as fully participating citizens.

Self determination is not the same thing as self sufficiency. Someone does not have to be entirely self sufficient in order to be self determining. The degree of support that a person might need has no bearing on his right to self determination or on his capacity to be self determining. In fact, someone might require a great deal of practical assistance and still be very capable of making his own decisions and directing his own supports. At the same time, few people make all of their own decisions completely autonomously, and in fact most of us are influenced in our decision-making by our family, our spouse, our employer, our friends. So even those who consider themselves to be self-determining will likely need support, as we all do, from time to time.

Self-determination isn't simply about people doing whatever they want, with no regard for the impact of their choices on others or on their own circumstances. We've heard examples of staff standing by while someone emptied his bank account on a whim, or sending someone out in the cold without proper footwear or clothing, in the name of supporting the person's self-determination (*"Terry chose to spend his holiday savings on a new computer"*). People who haven't had much choice or control in their lives will need to build up their experience with choice-making and learn how to make informed choices by weighing the pros and cons of a situation, researching their options, getting advice from people they know and trust, etc. With authority comes responsibility for one's choices, and again, people who haven't had many opportunities to learn about responsibility will need to practice this. It isn't reasonable to expect someone who's never been given any real responsibility to suddenly be expected to stand accountable for spending his hard-earned savings on a whim.

Some ways to support self determination:

- Always involve people in discussions / decisions that affect them;
- Provide frequent opportunities for choice-making;
- Practice problem-solving, for example making pro / con lists as a way to consider the implications of different options or choices;
- Encourage people to speak for themselves – don't speak for them;
- Have high expectations – convey confidence in the person;
- Acknowledge the person's accomplishments, celebrate successes;
- Honour the person's story, and understand where people are coming from – offer to help the person write their story, keep a journal, make photo albums or scrapbooks;

- Teach people about rights and responsibilities;
- Use plain language, not jargon – advocate for access to information in ways the person can understand, eg. medical information;
- Prepare people for planning meetings, medical appointments, etc. – talk about what to expect, write down questions or concerns ahead of time, practice asking questions;
- Use age appropriate teaching methods – treat adults like adults, not children;
- Find opportunities for people to learn about self advocacy – eg. join a self advocacy group, subscribe to newsletters, attend conferences, talk to other self advocates;
- Support the person's initiative (ie. making choices or taking action without prompting);
- Find ways for the person to be a leader – eg. public speaking, teaching, mentoring opportunities;
- Allow for mistakes – don't over-protect or shield people from natural consequences;
- Treat mistakes as learning opportunities;
- Use positive language to describe the person – eg. "train hobbyist" instead of "obsessed with trains," "extroverted" as opposed to "attention seeking";
- Teach problem-solving skills and support people in solving their own problems – resist the temptation to take over;
- Promote reasonable risk taking – facilitate a discussion with the person and her team about what constitutes *reasonable risk;*
- Praise the person's self expression – encourage people to develop their own style, have their own opinions and tastes

Self advocacy

Self advocacy refers to people with disabilities speaking up for their rights and advocating for themselves. It is an important aspect of self determination.

The self advocacy movement can trace its roots to British Columbia, where the first conference for people with developmental disabilities in North America was held in 1973. Barb Goode, who was at that conference and went on to start the first Canadian chapter of *People First*, remembers what it was like for people with developmental disabilities starting to find their voice as self advocates:

"It wasn't easy being a self-advocate in those days. It still isn't, I guess. I remember this one time back then when we were invited to a meeting with people who were not handicapped. It was the first time our People First group had been invited to a meeting like this. Right away, I noticed that the others like me weren't talking at all, and no one was inviting them to – so I did. Well, I felt like some of the non-handicapped people...were upset that I had been so honest and outspoken. They thought it was wrong for me to speak up. I feel it is this attitude of superiority from some people that creates the biggest stumbling blocks to our acceptance in the community." (Goode, 2011)

Norma Collier, a parent and past president of BCACL, recalls:

"From a retrospective point of view, the main achievement of [the 1970s] was the beginnings of change in consciousness regarding the possible abilities of our labeled sons and daughters and our responses to them. As we took bold steps forward on their behalf, we were rewarded and amazed by their obvious desire to do more and more." (Collier, 1995)

Barb would say an important aspect of self advocacy is using language that people with developmental disabilities can understand, because information is power. She talks about the importance of making information accessible to people with low literacy through the use of *plain language*, and using *people first* language (referring to the person first and the disability second):.

"Defective became insane became retarded became mentally retarded became mentally handicapped became developmentally delayed became intellectually challenged became people with mental handicaps became people with disabilities. See how long it took for people to come before disability." (Goode, 2011).

Person-centred planning

In B.C., there's now a mandatory course called Planning 10 that all high school students must take to satisfy graduation requirements. Its purpose is "to enable students to develop the skills they need to become self-directed individuals who set goals, make thoughtful decisions, and take responsibility for pursuing their goals throughout life." (Ministry of Education website).

While it's probably not the Ministry's expectation that 15 year olds will emerge from this course fully self-determined and ready to plan the rest of their lives, the idea that everyone has a sense of purpose in life and that achieving one's vision of a good life requires some intentional effort is one that resonates for most people nowadays. It's a relatively new idea though. In generations past, role expectancies were more narrowly delineated than they are today. Fifty years ago, it wasn't uncommon for young women to leave high school, get married and start a family. If they chose to work, their employment options were much more limited than they are today. Young men, on the other hand, were expected to get a good job that would allow them to support a family. Boys took auto shop and industrial education in high school, where girls studied home economics. People with developmental disabilities weren't expected to become self supporting, or to get married and have families (they were actually discouraged from doing so), and so the role expectancies for them were even more limited. Planning basically consisted of deciding which program they would be placed in ("*this sheltered workshop, or that one?*"), and which professional services they would have (speech therapy, occupational therapy, etc.).

In much the same way that the women's movement challenged assumptions about the role of women and opened up new opportunities beyond traditional employment, educational and gender roles, the community living movement began to challenge assumptions about the roles and potential of people with developmental disabilities. Embracing the idea that people are capable of learning and of taking an active role in leading their own lives changes the ground rules for the whole system of human services. No longer is it considered acceptable for professionals to decide where people should live and what kinds of programs will be available to them. Like the girls in my high school who started asking to take woodworking class instead of sewing, people with developmental disabilities and their families started asking for more than the limited service options that were available to them ("*actually, I don't want a sheltered workshop, I want a real job*"). Just as the school system is recognizing the need to equip young people with skills for planning their futures, so the human service system is beginning to recognize the need to equip people with developmental disabilities and their allies with the skills for planning and directing their own lives. Our task in the new world order is to figure out how to work with people rather than doing for them, to follow their lead rather than taking over, to build flexible support arrangements that promote independence rather than boxing people into prescribed program placements and creating further dependence, to help people achieve a good life, not just acquire more services. This is the essence of person-centred planning.

The first community-based services adopted the same kind of planning practices that had been used in the institutions, with professionals deciding what was best for people and placing them in segregated programs based on their perceived level of functioning. Normalization and Social Role Valorization turned this thinking on its head. A handful of leaders in our field began to experiment with different approaches to planning that put the person at the centre, and considered what an optimal life could look like for the person, beyond the limited scope of available services and personnel. Over time, these approaches came to be referred to under the broad heading of person-centred planning, distinguishing them from the more traditional system-centred or program-centred planning. Traditional planning took a *deficits-based* approach, where the underlying question was *"what's wrong with this person, and how do we fix it?"* Person-centred planning, by contrast, takes a *strengths-based* approach. It asks the question, *"what does the person want her life to look like, and how can we help her get there?"* These kinds of questions don't lend themselves to a standardized approach, or even to a single meeting. Discovering one's strengths and gifts is a process that unfolds over time.

A variety of person-centred planning methodologies were developed during the 1980s, including Personal Futures Planning, MAPS, Circles of Support, PATH, and Essential Lifestyle Planning. There is a wealth of information and some excellent publications on person-centred planning, much of it written by those who pioneered these approaches a quarter century ago (O'Brien & Lyle-O'Brien, 1988; Falvey, Forest, Pearpoint & Rosenberg, 2000; Mount, 2000; O'Brien & Blessing, eds., 2011). While each approach has its unique elements, they share some common features that distinguish them from traditional approaches to planning:

Traditional planning	Person-centred planning
Planning occurs once a year, as an isolated event.	Planning is ongoing and fluid.
Planning generally happens in an office around a table, following a prescribed format.	Planning happens wherever it is most comfortable for the person, and can follow a variety of different formats.
Decision-making rests with staff and professionals.	Decision-making rests with the person and those closest to him or her.
Staff and professionals come up with a plan *for* the person.	Staff and professionals work in partnership *with* the person.
Planning is *deficits-based*, meaning it focuses on what the person is lacking.	Planning is *strengths-based*, meaning it focuses on the person's gifts and abilities.
Planning centres on supporting the person within a pre-defined program.	Planning centres on supporting the person to be fully engaged in community.
Planning results in a standardized written document (ISP, PSP, etc) that is considered fixed for a period of one year.	Planning results in action plans that are flexible and individualized. Ongoing revisions are to be expected.
Specialist and disability-related services are the first or only consideration for responding to the person's needs.	Generic supports and services are the first consideration, augmented by specialist or disability-related services only as necessary.

While person-centred planning isn't just about an annual meeting, nor is it simply about being in the moment with people. Staff sometimes believe they're being person-centred merely by offering people choices of this activity or that, in a kind of impromptu approach to community support where the sole purpose seems to be filling the person's day with activity. Adherents of this approach might even object to the notion of formalized planning or to enlisting other people's input to planning – *"I know the person best"* and *"we just go with the flow"* are the kinds of things people might say in defense of this kind of approach. Without a sense of purpose or a context for the activities we're engaging in, the danger is that people get stuck in a cycle of dependence; they become participants in their own lives, waiting for their staff to show up and entertain them. People who come to our organization for support are usually looking for more than leisure activities and companionship. They want to increase their independence, to expand their network of friends and community connections, to find a job, to create a home of their own – and while we are getting ever better at supporting these aspects of people's lives, the default of staff-directed leisure activities is an all too easy trap to fall into.

Agencies everywhere have adopted the language of person-centred planning, but often the process that gets implemented is not so different from planning of old. Good facilitation is key to good person-centred planning, and not just facilitating a meeting, but enlisting the right people to be part of the planning, asking the right questions, and following up to make sure people have the resources and support they need to put the plan into action. Planning doesn't end with the meeting, it's ongoing. It requires active, skilled facilitation from someone with the authority to protect and defend the plan from other competing interests.

Often the responsibility for planning falls to program managers, which can be problematic if they have other competing interests they need to satisfy. John Lord would argue that facilitation of person-centred planning should be done by someone from outside the team whose focus is squarely on the individual and who can think outside the box of existing support arrangements (Lord, Leavitt and Dingwall, 2012). An independent facilitator might bring a fresh set of eyes to planning, ask different questions, and elicit different kinds of responses. Let's say Laura has a dream of starting her own dog-walking business, but no-one on her team knows how to help her do this; or maybe her support hours are dedicated to other activities and there's no ability within the current schedule to support Laura to walk dogs. An independent facilitator might be more likely to look outside the parameters of the current staffing arrangement, and consider other ways or other people who could assist Laura to achieve her dream.

To be truly person-centred requires us to surrender control, to be open to ideas that might be very different from our own, and to learn how to follow rather than lead. Person-centred planning is a commitment to a way of being in relationship with the person, a commitment to person-centred thinking and action. It's an ambitious undertaking. It starts with having a clear vision of what *a good life* means to the person, and then thinking deeply about what needs to happen to begin to realize that vision. It requires us to move beyond planning for the routine tasks of daily living – housekeeping, nutrition, personal care – and think bigger, aspire to more. If we think back to John O'Brien's *Five Valued Experiences*, person-centred planning should focus our collective efforts and resources in support of building good lives in community, where people experience belonging, respect, sharing of ordinary spaces, contribution and choice.

The *Five Valued Experiences* tie to *Five Service Accomplishments,* which speak to the intentionality of person-centred planning as an opportunity to reflect on the support arrangements we've put in place and to think about the impact our support is having on people's lives:

> "Service workers who want to assist people with disabilities to get or keep out of the box have to build alliances that are strong enough and plans that are imaginative enough to energize creative action that opens pathways for people's energy, capacities, and gifts to flow into community life. They continue to improve the quality of their answers to the questions that define the **five accomplishments.**
>
> *How can we assist people to make and sustain connections, memberships and friendships?* Service workers make a difference when they listen deeply and act thoroughly to provide exactly what a person needs to build a bridge to community participation.
>
> *How do we enhance people's reputation?* Respect comes to those who play recognizable and valued parts in everyday life. Service workers make a difference when they support people to identify and take up social roles that express their interests and provide needed assistance with negotiating the accommodations they need to be successful and so encourage valued social roles.
>
> *How do we increase people's active involvement in the life of our communities?* Service workers make a difference when they assist people to make the most of the ordinary community settings that attract their interest and energy. This increases community presence.
>
> *How do we assist people to develop and invest their gifts and capacities?* Service workers make a difference when they focus on what each person can bring to others and bring imagination and technical competence to designing and delivering the help each person needs to develop competence.

How do we increase choice and control in people's lives? Service workers make a difference when they honor people's rights and responsibilities and offer what works to promote their autonomy." (O'Brien, 2011)

Reducing person-centred planning to an annual bureaucratic exercise, or not doing it at all, makes it less likely that these accomplishments will be realized. It is possible to do good person-centred planning but not have that planning translate into a good life in community. To paraphrase the poet Robert Burns, the best laid person-centred plans go awry if there's no commitment to follow through.

Goal-setting

Ongoing person-centred planning sets the stage for goal-setting that can help the person move closer to realizing his vision of a good life, and help his supporters to focus their time and energy on the things that are most important to the person.

Research shows that when we write down our goals, the chances of us following through are greater than if we don't write them down (Matthews, 2008). The act of writing down our goals forces us to get clear on what exactly it is we want to accomplish, and to think through the steps we can take to get there. Setting clear goals helps translate the person's vision into action, and creates forward momentum. Goal-setting can be beneficial to the person in many ways:

- Builds confidence – experiencing success with one goal gives the person confidence to set a next goal, and a next. Small goals lead to more ambitious ones;
- Promotes self determination and self direction – having goals tells others that the person is in charge, that she has a plan and is actively pursuing it;
- Focuses time and resources on the things that matter most to the person;
- Provides opportunities for celebration – everyone loves to see people accomplish their goals. Celebrate those successes!

Goal setting is part of person-centred planning, and it should always be considered within that context. By definition, individual goals belong to the person – there should never be a time when staff are setting goals for people, without their input.

The activities we engage in with people on a day to day basis should align with their stated goals. If the person simply has a schedule of activities with no indication as to the purpose of the activities, then staff are left to guess at how best to support the person. Let's say Cindy goes to the library every Wednesday as part of her weekly routine. The purpose of the library outing might be to look at books, or it might be to get to know the library staff and some of the other regular customers as a way to build Cindy's network, or it might be to improve her literacy skills. It could be that one of Cindy's staff started taking her to the library years ago because that staff person liked going to the library, and even though that person is no longer working with Cindy, the routine has continued. Maybe Cindy doesn't even like going to the library!

If an activity is important enough to be part of a person's weekly schedule, then it should reflect the priorities she's expressed through the process of person-centred planning, and everyone who assists her with the activity should be clear on its intended purpose. Those who accompany Cindy to the library should be able to explain how going to the library ties in to the overall direction of Cindy's life, to her overall plan.

SMART goals

SMART is an acronym for specific, measurable, achievable, realistic and time-limited. Writing SMART goals is a useful strategy for clarifying the scope and purpose of an activity or task. Often we see people setting vague goals, like *"making more friends"* or *"being more active"* that might mean completely different things to different people, and are therefore difficult to track. How will we know when the goal of *"being more active"* has been met? With SMART goals, we can take a big goal and break it down into smaller goals that allow the person to experience success in incremental steps. Accomplishing one goal, celebrating it, and moving on to another, perhaps more challenging goal, builds momentum and gives the person a sense of accomplishment.

An example of a SMART goal related to Cindy's library outing might be:

"By April, Cindy will have joined a book club," or, even better, from Cindy's perspective:

"By April, I will have joined a book club."

Cindy can then share her goals with new people who come to support her, which will create opportunities for her to be self-directing. She might also want to share her goal with the staff at the library, and with her friends and family, so they know what it is she's working towards and can help her achieve her goal. Chances are, someone will know someone who belongs to a book club that Cindy could join. The possibility of success greatly increases when Cindy's goal is articulated and shared with others. The chances of Cindy finding a book club if it's just Cindy and her staff quietly visiting the library every Wednesday are not nearly so great. The chance of finding a book club if her staff don't even know that's what Cindy wants is probably nil.

Dignity of risk

"Many of our best achievements came the hard way: we took risks, fell flat, suffered, picked ourselves up, and tried again. Sometimes we made it and sometimes we did not. Even so, we were given the chance to try. [People with developmental disabilities] need these chances too." (Perske, 1981)

Many of the things people identified as being important for a good life involve an element of risk: one cannot experience love without risking the pain of loss; we can't go out and apply for work without risking rejection, and so on. In fact, "taking risks" was itself identified by our group of self advocates as an indicator of a good life. Many people with disabilities we talk to say they feel under-challenged and over-protected in their day-to-day lives. They say that others sometimes impose restrictions on them that would not be considered reasonable for anyone else, under the guise of keeping them safe. The idea that people are safer if we shelter them from any and all potential dangers is misguided. The intention might be good – we don't want to see people get hurt – but ironically, when we over-protect people we actually put them at greater risk. What happens when we're not there, or when people venture into new or unfamiliar situations? People need to learn how to recognize danger, and to acquire and practice skills for keeping themselves safe.

A few months ago, I came across a clip from a television show featuring Rick Hansen. He was bungee jumping. The Man in Motion, who raised millions of dollars for spinal cord research wheeling around the world, was strapped in his wheelchair to a harness above a 160-foot gorge, about to be pushed over the edge of the platform. I actually gasped out loud. *"Don't do it, Rick!"* I wanted to call out. And while that might well be my reaction to anyone about to jump off a platform into thin air, my impression of the heightened risk for someone in a wheelchair in this situation was probably shared by many viewers, even though such concerns might be completely unfounded. The people in charge of the bungee jumping operation didn't seem overly concerned, they simply strapped Mr. Hansen into the harness and then added a second harness to secure his wheelchair. They assessed the risk, and put appropriate safeguards in place.

The point isn't that we should ignore dangers or minimize threats to people's safety, but rather that we figure out how to balance *reasonable* risks with appropriate safeguards. How much risk we're comfortable supporting, and what kinds of risks people might take, will depend on each person's unique circumstances. The notion of *dignity of risk* is that each of us has the right to answer these questions in our own way, and we need to acknowledge that some of life's most important lessons are learned by taking risks.

Looking at individual needs

There's sometimes a reluctance on the part of supporters to talk about people's needs, as if focusing on needs will somehow present the person in a negative light, or detract from his strengths and gifts. It's important that we distinguish between *needs* and *deficiencies*. Needs can be thought of as the things we all require for a good life. Deficiencies, on the other hand, are generally thought of as weaknesses, or shortcomings. The old style of planning often focused on deficiencies, rather than needs – as in *"Ben has no language skills"* or *"Ben is non-verbal."* There was a presumption of incompetence, a view of the person as lacking in some way. Reframing Ben's communication as an area of need – as in *"Ben needs a reliable system of communication"* or *"Ben needs communication partners who share some of his interests"* – presumes competence, and offers a way forward. Needs are not inherently positive or negative, they're just the things we require to live a good life. It's our attribution of value to the need that determines whether it will be seen as a deficiency or an opportunity.

Michael Kendrick identifies 20 universal domains of need:

- Nutrition

- Health

- Home

- Work

- Financial Viability

- Autonomy

- Value, Reputation And Respect

- Valued Social Roles And Images

- Social Inclusion

- Mobility

- Vulnerabilities And Safeguards

- Learning, Growth And Experiences

- Transport

- Non Vocational/Leisure

- Communication

- Meaning/Spirituality

- Identity And Culture

- Adaptive Devices

- Relationships

- Respect For And Exercise Of Rights

While everyone has needs in these domains, the relative importance of one need over another, and the degree to which each of these needs is satisfied, will vary greatly from one person to the next. If I have no food allergies or sensitivities, and no special dietary requirements, then my nutrition needs might not figure prominently in my planning; but if I develop an allergy to dairy products, all of a sudden my nutrition needs become more of a concern. My needs in the area of meaning and spirituality will be different from someone else's, or may be more or less of a focus for me at different times in my life.

Most of the needs that someone with a developmental disability has are the same kinds of needs anyone else has – perhaps manifested in different ways, but the same underlying needs. It stands to reason, then, that our preferred means of addressing people's needs should be the same means (*normative means*) that others of a similar age and culture would use. Sue, a fifty year old woman with cerebral palsy, will have needs that are more like those of other fifty year old women than like the needs of other people with cerebral palsy. She might also have a few specialized needs that other fifty year old women don't share, but for the most part, the optimal solution to meeting her needs will be the same kinds of solutions other women her age turn to. If Sue needs more friends, she might like to join a women's social group or take part in a retreat with other women her age.

The service system, however, often has the opposite impulse. It responds to typical needs in atypical ways. For example, we might respond to Sue's need for friendship by sending her to a social group for people with disabilities, ignoring the many similar needs Sue shares with other women her age and focusing instead on the few specialized needs she might share with other people with disabilities.

One of our favourite examples of a normative response comes from an agency we did some work with in a rural community in the interior of B.C.. Janet, a woman they supported, was looking forward to starting her new job at a hardware store. The only problem – it was in the next town, about 50 km from where she lived. Her support worker contacted the company that provides specialized transportation services in the area, and attempted to arrange Janet's transportation to and from her new job, but she was told they wouldn't be able to accommodate Janet's needs. The agency's first impulse was to appeal to the head of the transportation service, but then someone asked, "what would the normative solution be?" What would you or I do if we needed transportation to and from work in another town? Someone suggested car-pooling. The staff discovered that one of Janet's new co-workers lived fairly close to her, so she approached the woman to see if she'd consider having Janet car-pool with her in exchange for gas money. The woman said she'd be happy to help out, and in fact she'd enjoy the company! It turned out Janet and her co-worker had a lot in common, and before long they became good friends.

Addressing Janet's transportation needs through normative means had the added benefit of addressing needs in other areas of her life, including relationships, value / respect, communication and social inclusion – needs that would not have been addressed to the same extent, if at all, with the specialized transportation option.

If we are to design services and supports that truly help people realize their vision of a good life, then we must seek to understand and address their needs across these various domains, and not limit our thinking to the most obvious or basic needs that the service system often focuses on.

Vulnerabilities and safeguards

Years ago, I heard Lou Brown speak at a conference about a boy he'd met early in his career as a special educator, a boy who had been born with no arms. When the boy entered the school system, he was placed in a special class and surrounded with specialized support: a full-time aide, occupational therapy, adaptive equipment, special seating at his own table. Reflecting back years later, Dr. Brown concluded, *"we let him down."* The boy never made any friends, he never took part in any clubs or teams during his time at school. He had been kept safe, at least insofar as his physical needs had been met. A decade or so later, Dr. Brown was called in to consult at a school in another state. A child had moved into the district and was starting school that fall. A child who had been born without arms. The school wanted Dr. Brown's help to figure out how to support this child in their special education program. His advice: place the child in a regular class. *"The best therapy for kids with disabilities is other kids,"* he said. True, the child would need some special equipment and support, but even more than that, he would need friends. And the other students – his peers who would one day be employers and neighbours and landlords and doctors in the adult world he'd be part of – needed to grow up knowing this boy and seeing him as belonging with them, in community, and not somewhere separate.

We often think of vulnerabilities in terms of a person's physical care, as in a health issue that makes a person susceptible to infections, or mobility limitations that make a person vulnerable to falling. So we take care, quite rightly, to put safeguards in place that minimize obvious dangers to the person's physical well-being. However people can be vulnerable in many different ways. For example someone living in a home with people who don't fully understand or appreciate his needs is going to be more vulnerable to abuse or neglect than someone living with people of his own choosing who have authentic, caring relationships with the person. Someone with limited education and work experience is going to be more vulnerable to unemployment or under-employment, and more at risk for a life of poverty, than someone with more education and work experience. Someone who spends all her time with paid people and has no friends or unpaid others in her life is going to be more vulnerable by virtue of her dependence on the service system than someone with a rich network of people in her life: more vulnerable to abuse and neglect, more lonely, more deeply wounded when one of her supporters leaves and is replaced by someone new.

Looking beyond the person's obvious or outward vulnerabilities is an important aspect of good person-centred planning. If we look back at Michael Kendrick's domains of need, we can imagine how unmet needs in any area could heighten a person's vulnerability. For example if Ben has a need for augmentative communication and it goes unmet, he is going to be vulnerable to people not understanding him, or ignoring his attempts at communication.

People with disabilities might have the same vulnerabilities as anyone else, but it's also true that they might be more vulnerable, or experience *enhanced vulnerability*, depending on the opportunities they have in life, or the lack thereof:

> "Enhanced vulnerability happens because people with disabilities are more likely to experience disadvantages in life and often have fewer opportunities. This comes from factors such as having less money, limited access to resources, fewer friends and close relationships. It also comes from negative treatment by others...[and] the low value that many people in society place on the lives of people with disabilities." (CLBC, 2009)

Putting appropriate safeguards in place to address each person's unique vulnerabilities is critical. The focus, however, should be on *personal* safeguards, not just programmatic or one-size-fits-all safeguards. The assumption in some of our traditional service models is that people might not have a lot of control, but at least they're safe, what with bathing protocols and menu plans and set bedtimes and all. The belief is that if we have enough rules, and apply them consistently, everyone will be safe. But when we restrict people's choices, we rob them of their personal freedom, which, in turn, makes them more vulnerable. There might be one person in the program who is known to wander into traffic, and so a rule is established that no-one is allowed to go out without staff. Or someone turned the stove on once and forgot to turn it off, so now nobody is allowed to use the stove without supervision.

Through person-centred planning, we look at each individual's unique needs and vulnerabilities, and then build personal safeguards that make sense for each person. If being near busy streets puts Kathy at risk of being hit by a car, we build in safeguards to address this vulnerability when she's out and about. If Gordon needs to be within visual or hearing range of someone at all times because of his seizure disorder, we make sure he has people close by who know how to respond when he has a seizure. Unfortunately, if Kathy only ever goes out with a group of people, everyone else ends up being closely watched around traffic, whether they need this level of vigilance or not. If Gordon shares a home with others who are able to be alone for periods of time, they might never get the opportunity to be by themselves because there are staff on-site 24 hours a day tending to Gordon. These are not insurmountable challenges, but they highlight the need for thoughtful planning for each person to ensure that safeguards we put in place for one person don't infringe on the rights and freedoms of others.

Safeguards come in all shapes and sizes. They range from simple things like having locks on doors to the more sophisticated, like video surveillance. Safeguards can be formal or informal. *Formal safeguards* are things we do with intention – for example, having identification with us when we travel, or carrying a fanny pack with emergency medication. *Informal safeguards* are things we do as a natural part of our day, that are so ingrained in our behaviour we might not consciously think, *"this is helping me to stay safe"* – for example, getting enough sleep, exercise, and nutritious food every day, or staying on public walkways when we're out alone and avoiding isolated, poorly lit areas.

Most of the safeguards we use in our day-to-day lives are informal. But often when we think about safeguards for people with disabilities, our tendency is to look for formal safeguards first – things like staff coverage, fire drills, supervised outings. A different way (a more person-centred way) to approach the question of safeguards is to look at all of the informal safeguards the person has in his life already, and be more intentional about using them. For example, instead of scheduling staff to pick Josh up after work and bring him home, maybe there's a co-worker who gets along well with Josh and who would be happy to drive him home. *"But..."* you're thinking, *"what if Josh's co-worker is sick one day, or what if he forgets to drive Josh home one day?"* Well, what would any of us do if we were stranded and needed a ride home? We'd call a cab, or we'd walk, or take transit. We'd summon up an alternative from our repertoire of informal safeguards, and we'd figure it out. We can help Josh build his own repertoire by being *intentional* about identifying and tapping informal safeguards that speak to his unique vulnerabilities. Plan A might be for Josh's co-worker to drive him home, but we also build in backup plans in case Plan A doesn't happen. Plan B could be that Josh carries a

$20 bill in an envelope to use as emergency cab fair if he needs it, and Plan C could be carrying a cell phone so he can call home if he's stranded, and so on.

The table below shows some examples of personal safeguards that might be put in place to address particular vulnerabilities.

Vulnerability	Possible Safeguards
Karen wants to go to the mall with her friends, but she's never been without her parents or support worker and they are concerned that she might get lost.	Go with Karen to the mall to make sure she connects with her friends, and then arrange to meet up with her later at a specified time and place. A backup safeguard could be for Karen to carry a cell phone and practice calling home, or her parents could call her.
Bryce likes to hug everyone he meets. This makes some people uncomfortable and not want to be close to him. It also makes him vulnerable to teasing and bullying.	Teach Bryce to shake hands instead of hugging people he doesn't know. Make up personalized business cards that he can carry with him and hand out to people as another way of introducing himself.
Wendy likes to help in the kitchen but her impulsivity puts her at risk of burning herself on the stove or cutting herself with a sharp utensil.	Set up tasks that Wendy can do sitting down at the kitchen table. Get a pair of safe kitchen shears so she can cut vegetables instead of chopping them with a knife.

Relationships

"We have only begun to sense the tragic wounds that so many [people with developmental disabilities] may feel when it dawns on them that the only people relating to them – outside of relatives – are paid to do so. If you or I came to such a sad realization about ourselves, it would rip at our souls to even talk about it." (Perske, 1988)

People consistently rank relationships at or near the top of the list of indicators for what constitutes a good quality of life. Human beings are social creatures. Relationships give our lives meaning and purpose. Having a network of family, friends, neighbours, co-workers and others who know and care about us not only enhances our quality of life, it's also good for our health. A 2010 study by psychologists at Brigham Young University looked at the impact of social relationships on physical and mental health, and concluded:

"Individuals with adequate social relationships have a 50% greater likelihood of survival compared to those with poor or insufficient social relationships. The magnitude of this effect is comparable to quitting smoking and it exceeds many well-known risk factors for mortality (e.g., obesity, physical inactivity)." (Holt-Lunstad, Smith & Layton, 2010).

And yet, our services often focus much more on addressing physical and material needs than on people's need for relationships. I've been at staff meetings over the years where the agenda was entirely to do with housekeeping (*"the groceries were over budget again last month," "the bathroom faucet needs fixing"*). If relationships were on the agenda at all, it was often about problems between the staff and families, as in *"how can we get Mrs. Sweeney to follow through on Lisa's diet when she goes home on the weekends?"* or *"John's sister dropped by again without calling ahead – we need to set some boundaries with her."*

It's interesting to see what happens by simply putting relationships at the top of the agenda for team meetings, to spend some time talking about who's in the person's life, what's going well with their relationships, and what more might be done to support this aspect of the person's life. By talking about relationships for even a few minutes before getting into the rest of the agenda, the whole tone of the conversation starts to shift. Instead of focusing on how to get Lisa's mom to follow her diet plan, someone might say, *"why don't we invite Lisa's mom for dinner on Sunday"* – because by the time they get to that part of the agenda, the meeting has been framed in the context of supporting relationships, as opposed to fixing problems. The question of

John's sister coming by unannounced gets reframed from a problem into an opportunity: *"John really enjoys spending time with his sister – maybe she'd like to go to the movies with him one night?"*

Sometimes staff might feel it's too much work to build relationships, or they don't have enough time because they're busy attending to other things, to other parts of their job. But building relationships doesn't have to take more time. Sometimes it's a matter of looking at what we're already doing and going about it in a different way. Many of our own relationships come about through our participation in ordinary, everyday activities – we meet people at work, at school, in our community – most of us don't set aside time to go out and build our relationships, it's just something that happens by virtue of the environments and activities we're part of. The same logic applies to people we support, we might just need to be a bit more intentional about recognizing the opportunities in everyday situations. John Lord talks about looking at everything we do through the "lens of relationship," by which he means that instead of looking at the activities and tasks of daily living as things to be completed and checked off a list, we can look at them as opportunities for deepening and expanding the person's relationships. So instead of thinking of grocery shopping strictly in terms of its practical value (re-stocking the kitchen cupboards), we can think of it as an opportunity for connection, like Walter and his support worker did:

Walter had a reputation as someone with extremely challenging behaviour, to the point that we had a hard time finding and keeping staff to work with him. Most of our time and energy with Walter was spent keeping him safe, keeping him from damaging the furniture and punching holes in the walls of his home, and keeping his roommate out of harm's way. Walter had lived in an institution for 40 years before we met him, with very little exposure to the community or to the typical activities of daily living, like grocery shopping. He enjoyed going with his staff to the grocery store every week, and while this could be challenging at times (like when Walter would help himself to a snack off one of the shelves or climb onto a counter to reach something off a display board), the benefits to Walter of being part of this activity far outweighed the occasional tense moments.

It wasn't long before Walter and his staff became familiar faces at the store, and one cashier in particular took a strong interest in Walter. His support worker started making a point of taking Walter shopping on the days when this cashier was working, and going to her check-out line.

Over time, she started greeting Walter with a hug, which he clearly enjoyed, and wanting to know more about him – where did he live, and could she come visit him sometime? Again, the staff made a point of following up and shortly thereafter she came over for a visit. A few months later she came to his birthday party. At Christmas, she came by with gifts, and invited Walter to come for dinner at her house.

Years later at Walter's funeral, his dear friend, the grocery store cashier, gave a moving tribute to him, saying how he had enriched her life in so many ways. This man, who we literally couldn't pay people to spend time with, and who no-one ever expected to have friends, had touched someone's life in a way none of us could have predicted or planned for. There was no question that this was the most significant relationship of Walter's life, outside of his immediate family, and it came about through the unlikely activity of grocery shopping, because his staff looked at this activity through the lens of relationship.

Building personal networks

In 2007, our agency was selected to take part in a demonstration project funded by Community Living British Columbia (CLBC) that looked at the personal support networks – relationships with family, friends, neighbours and unpaid others – of people with developmental disabilities in various parts of the province. Along with three other agencies, we spent six months working with individuals who had expressed a desire to expand or deepen their relationships, to see what was getting in the way of building strong networks, and what could be done to overcome some of the barriers. The learning from this project was summarized in a report entitled Belonging to One Another: Building personal support networks, which is available on the CLBC website. Some of the insights from this project were:

- People with developmental disabilities want the same kinds of relationships as everyone else. They want friends, they want to be part of their extended family and to have valued roles as siblings and aunts and uncles, they want to love and be loved. For almost everyone we talked to, relationships were at the top of their list of priorities;
- Communities are full of people who are looking for connection, people who want more friends. This isn't a disability-specific issue, it's a community issue, and people with developmental disabilities have much to offer when it comes to addressing it;

- Our services sometimes get in the way of natural relationships, either by pushing unpaid others away or by creating barriers to inclusion.

A personal network can be thought of as the web of connections we have to other people, and the various roles we play within those relationships. A big part of how we define ourselves is through our personal network: the people we live with, the people we work with, the people we socialize with, people who inspire and challenge us, people we confide in or call upon when we need a shoulder to cry on.

Most of us grew up as part of an extended network of family, friends, neighbours, school-mates, etc. and probably didn't put much thought into intentionally building our network. But for those who might have missed out on the usual opportunities for connecting with other people, the task of making friends and developing a sense of one's place in community might require some intentional effort.

Formal networks

A formal or *intentional* network is a group of people who come together around a person with a disability and make a commitment to work together in support of the person. This can be especially important for people whose sole support, outside of paid staff, is their parents – an all too common scenario for many people with developmental disabilities. Parents often feel like they're the only ones who have their son or daughter's interests at heart, and they worry what will happen when they're gone. At the same time, they don't want to impose on siblings, friends or extended family. Even if they know of people who might like a more active role in their son or daughter's life, they don't know how to ask, or what to ask them to do. We're part of a culture that values self sufficiency. We don't like asking for help.

For these reasons, a facilitator might need to take the lead in organizing an intentional network. There are many different ways this can happen, depending on the purpose and composition of the network. For example, someone might have a need for a circle of friends, a network of committed people who come together with the intention of supporting the person over the long term, as friends and advocates. Or the focus might be bringing people together for a specified period of time or to assist with a particular task, such as helping the person to plan a move or find a job. Generally a facilitator will work with the person and his family to get the network up and running, and in some cases may continue to have a formal role facilitating network meetings.

Circles

One way to begin to look at personal networks is by mapping out the different layers, or "circles" of relationships in a person's life. This approach, developed by Jack Pierpoint, Marsha Forest and Judith Snow, looks at relationships as a series of concentric rings around the focal person, representing different layers of relationships:

> *Intimacy* – the inner circle, or our closest relationships – typically a spouse, parents, children, best friend
>
> *Friendship* – the next layer of relationship is our friends (might also include family or extended family members who we wouldn't necessarily include in our intimate circle)
>
> *Participation* – people we see on a regular basis or share a particular activity with, but are not necessarily friends
>
> *Economic exchange* – the outer circle, furthest away from us, is for the people who are paid to be in our life – eg. our doctor, counsellor, teachers, employer

> (Adapted from Bunch, Finnegan & Pearpoint, 2009)

What this exercise often reveals is that people with developmental disabilities might have more people in their outer circle (economic exchange) and fewer in the inner circles – in other words, more people who are paid to be in their life than people who are there voluntarily. This is opposite from what most of us experience. However, it's also common for people to have many names in their "participation" circle – people they know by name or see frequently, but aren't (yet) friends with. If there's even one name that jumps out as someone the person might like to get to know better, that's one potential new friend.

If people don't have a network, then it's important that we think about how we might help them build one. In our experience, when we do some digging, we always find people – family members we didn't know about, friends from school that the person has lost touch with, people from their neighbourhood. And we've been surprised at how easy it is to connect with people, when we get past the initial discomfort of taking that first step.

Some ways to support relationships

- Find out who is in the person's life – know who's important to the person and what their involvement is (or could be);
- Put "relationships" on the agenda for team meetings – make it a recurring topic;
- Assist people to keep track of their friends and family – have an address book, make photo albums, keep in touch with phone calls and visits, send birthday cards;
- Support the person to learn about social media, use email, etc.;
- Practice hospitality – find opportunities to be a host, practice greeting people;
- Practice reciprocity – give and take in relationships, conversation skills, active listening;
- Recognize barriers, and work to overcome them – for example, staffing schedules that limit the person's time with family and friends, or transportation barriers;
- Become "regulars" – visit the same places, at the same time, and get to know other regulars;
- Learn from the example of others – notice people with great social skills and watch what they do. Spend time in social spaces where people connect with each other;
- For more ideas on building relationships, check out 101 Ways to Make Friends (Johannes & Stanfield, 2011) and 101 Ways to Facilitate Making Friends (Johannes, Reynolds & Stanfield, 2011).

Home

"I always wanted my own place. [In the institution] it's not like a real home. They make you go to bed at 6:00 even if you're not tired. You don't get to make your own choices; everything is decided for you. Sometimes people didn't listen to me so I just stopped talking. It was awful. I wanted to get out so bad but they said I couldn't live in the community. Finally I got out and now I live in my own apartment with [my roommate]. I get to choose who supports me. I like having friends over to visit and having parties. I'm so happy to finally have my own place." – Barb

The longing for home is universal. Everyone, regardless of age, income, culture or ability, yearns for a place to call home, a place where they are accepted and valued without question. Home is much more than the physical space we occupy: it's a feeling of belonging, a safe haven, a sanctuary. Home is the place we leave each morning and return to at the end of the day, secure in the knowledge that whatever chaos might be going on in the world outside, we can close the door and get away from it all. We can rest, unwind, rejuvenate, and be ourselves.

In the past, many people with developmental disabilities were taken from their homes and placed in institutions, which are about as opposite from anyone's notion of home as you can get. When the institutions started downsizing and people came back into community, many were again "placed" into housing that was intended to be more like a real home. The idea was that reducing the number of people who lived together – from 60 people on a ward to four or five in a group home – would make for a more natural kind of living situation. In some cases, this might well have occurred, but in many others the result was what can best be described as mini-institutions, where people continued to be seen primarily as service recipients being cared for by staff and professionals, and where the regimentation of the old custodial model continued. Group homes may be more "home-like" than big institutions, but for most of us, "home-like" wouldn't be enough, and indeed for most of the people with developmental disabilities we meet, "home-like" isn't enough. They want a real home, not a placement in a residential service.

Whose home is it, anyway?

We're seeing the beginnings of a shift away from congregate models of housing to smaller, more personalized living arrangements. Having one or two people live together, instead of four or five, is a step in the right direction, but we need to be mindful about how we proceed, so as not to create even smaller mini-institutions. Individualizing the service does not guarantee a better quality of life for the person, nor does it automatically satisfy the person's need for *home*.

John O'Brien identifies three dimensions of home:

1.   *Sense of place*

   People are comfortable and secure in their home; they feel like they belong. They choose how they want to spend their time and who they spend it with. They contribute freely to the household and have a sense of pride in their home.

2.   *Control*

   People choose where they live, who they live with, and who provides them with needed supports. People have control over their own finances and decision-making, to the greatest extent possible.

3.   *Ownership or tenancy*

   People own or rent their own home, and occupy a valued social role as homeowner or tenant. (Adapted from O'Brien, 1991)

There are many different residential service models, each with its own assumptions about home ownership and the respective roles and responsibilities of various parties. There's been a rapid expansion in the shared living model, where a person with a disability lives with a contracted caregiver, usually in the caregiver's home but sometimes the person owns the home and has a caregiver come and live in. If the person truly shares the home and is valued as an equal member of the household, it can be a great experience for everyone involved. But if the person is seen primarily as a lodger or as a guest in someone else's home, then it can quickly start to feel more like a placement and less like home.

The chart below shows some of the ways we distinguish home from a residential service:

Residential service	Home
The person occupies a bed or a vacancy in a specially designed resource, often with people of a wide range of ages	The person has an individualized living arrangement that reflects the range of options typical for people of the same age
The residence is referred to by its geographic location or by an agency / accounting code, eg. *Sherbrooke House,* or *Program 7.*	The home is referred to as the person's home, eg. *John's place*
The person is viewed as a resident / client / person in care	The person is viewed as a homeowner / renter / neighbor
Funding is attached to the residence – if people move out, the funding stays with the residence	Funding is individualized / portable – if people want to move, they take their funding with them
Furnishings and decor are chosen by the agency or staff	Furnishings and decor are chosen by the person
The person's stay in the residence is contingent on compliance with agency or house rules	The person is free to live as he or she chooses, within normative constraints
Household routines are determined by the staff or agency (meals, chores, bedtimes)	Household routines are determined by the person, or shared with roommates as equals
The service provider's presence is evident in the home – binders, office space, etc	The service provider's presence is not evident, or is kept to a minimum
Lack of opportunity and space for privacy / intimacy	Opportunities and space for privacy / intimacy
The person has little or no say over who enters the residence	The person decides who enters their home
Restrictions on guests / visitors	The person is free to have guests / visitors

Some ways to promote a sense of "home"

- Visit other home-owners / renters – see how other people live and talk to them about what home means to them;

- Refer to the person's home as a home, not a residential facility, eg. *Janet's home* as opposed to *West 14th House*;

- Deal with administrative or agency business off-site as much as possible;

- Assist the person to add personal touches to the home – display pictures of family, awards, souvenirs, mementos;

- Understand the person's culture / heritage / religion, and find ways to embed these in the home, eg. meals, rituals, celebrations;

- Respect personal space as belonging to the person: knock before coming in, ask permission before using the person's belongings or inviting others into the home;

- Encourage the person to decorate their home in ways that reflect their personal style and tastes – plants, pictures, furnishings, paint / wallpaper;

- Support the person to entertain family and friends of their choosing;

- Practice being a good neighbour – be a positive presence in the neighbourhood;

- Assist the person with home maintenance and upkeep – promote a sense of pride in the person's home;

- Practise hospitality – hosting dinners, movie nights, having people over for coffee

Employment

Article 27 of the UN Convention on the Rights of Persons with Disabilities recognizes the right of people with disabilities "to work, on an equal basis with others; this includes the right to the opportunity to gain a living by work freely chosen or accepted in a labour market and work environment that is open, inclusive and accessible to persons with disabilities." (UN Convention, 2006)

Much has been written about the benefits of paid employment for people with developmental disabilities (Mcloughlin et al, 1987; Wehman, 2007; CACL, 2011). Few things are valued more in our society than having a job. Aside from the obvious financial benefits, being employed gives people a sense of purpose, the chance to contribute to the economy, and it's often where people make friends. Working is also good for your health. A major study out of the United Kingdom looked at the relative impact of working vs. not working on physical and mental health and concluded:

> "There is a strong evidence base showing that work is generally good for physical and mental health and well-being. Worklessness is associated with poorer physical and mental health and well-being.... The provisos are that account must be taken of the nature and quality of work and its social context; jobs should be safe and accommodating. Overall, the beneficial effects of work outweigh the risks of work, and are greater than the harmful effects of long-term unemployment." (Waddell & Burton, 2006)

And yet, many people with developmental disabilities continue to be excluded from the workforce. In fact, people with developmental disabilities have among the lowest rates of employment in Canada at just over 25% (CACL, 2011).

Sheltered workshops were the main employment option for people with developmental disabilities in the past. These were large, segregated facilities, where people would do piece work or assembly line work for nominal pay. Sometimes there wasn't enough work to keep everyone busy, and so the staff would create make-work activity for people – I remember visiting a workshop once where the staff would un-package items at the end of the assembly line and send them back to the head of the line to be packaged again, just to keep people busy on slow days – or the workers would bide their time until the bus came to take them home. Our friend John was known to arrive at his workshop each morning, head straight to the back room, and plant himself on the couch, sleeping away most of the day. He did this for years. On the plus side, he still got paid the $60/month stipend that everyone else at the workshop earned, just for showing up.

As the community living movement progressed, more youth with disabilities who had grown up in community started coming into adult services, and with them came calls for a wider range of employment options. Supported employment emerged in the 1980s, in keeping with changing attitudes regarding the potential of people with developmental disabilities, and concerns about the lack of productivity in sheltered workshops and a lack of advancement from sheltered workshops into real work. The workshops, like the institutions before them, had become over-crowded, forcing service providers either to relocate to larger buildings, open more of them, or figure out how to start transitioning people out of them. In B.C., the issue was largely resolved for them when the Employment Standards Act changed in the 1990s, extending minimum wage regulations to workers in such facilities, which put most of the sheltered workshops out of business. Unfortunately, many service providers simply converted their facilities into non-vocational day activity centres, replacing the assembly line work with arts and crafts and karaoke. Gina, who was in her twenties when her service provider closed the sheltered workshop she'd been attending, recalls, "When the sheltered workshop closed, we all moved over to the day program. I've been there ever since. All I ever wanted was to get a job. The workshop wasn't great but at least there I was doing something and getting paid a bit of money. Now I'm not working at all."

Most people in our culture work, and are expected to work. The question for most of us isn't whether we work or not, but rather what type of work we will do. Most of the adults with developmental disabilities we meet tell us they want to be working. In recent years, some jurisdictions have committed to moving away from day activity programs to a re-focus on supported employment. Recently B.C. embraced an "Employment First" approach, whereby the first and most preferred outcome of community inclusion services should be employment. Employment First challenges the prevailing assumption of non-work as the default for adults with developmental disabilities and work as the exception. Instead, it says, the presumption should be that everyone will work. If some people choose not to work, that's their right, but non-work should be the exception, not the rule:

"Employment first is a concept and a practice which presupposes that all individuals with developmental disabilities, given adequate supports, can obtain and sustain integrated competitive employment. Employment First aligns with the vital concept of self-determination" (NACDD, 2011).

Some ways to promote "Employment First":

- Do an *asset inventory* of the person's skills, talents and strengths – an exhaustive list of all the things the person knows how to do or enjoys doing;

- Do a *community inventory* – walk through the person's neighbourhood and map out all of the places where people gather, the businesses, recreation centres, parks, schools, etc. Think about the kinds of work that gets done in these places and possible unmet needs or niche employment opportunities;

- Be curious – ask people what kind of work they might like to do; talk about different kinds of jobs that people do. Asking questions and being curious about the person's employment goals tells the person you see him as someone who is capable of working;

- Tell others that the person is looking for work – talk it up among the person's network;

- Ask family and friends what ideas they might have – invite their input, ask for personal referrals and contacts. Often people find work through personal contacts;

- Every day, do something related to looking for work or preparing for work – seek out opportunities to volunteer, collect reference letters, build skills that can be added to a resume;

- *Do what you love and the money will follow* – what is the person passionate about? Someone who loves animals might start a pet care business and offer to feed / walk / groom other people's pets when they're at work or when they're out of town;

- Get business cards printed with the person's contact information, and practice giving them to people who are potential employment contacts;

- Walk the walk – dress for success – practice the role;

- Find a mentor – someone who works in a field the person is interested in;

- Learn about supported employment and customized employment – attend conferences, read journal articles, find out what resources are out there, talk to other people who are working in supported or customized jobs

Competitive employment refers to the traditional employer-employee arrangement, where an employer advertises for a job, several applicants apply (or *compete*) for the job, and the most skilled or experienced person gets hired. There is generally some on-the-job training provided by the employer, but beyond that the employee is expected to perform the job independently, according to a set job description. With *supported employment,* the person gets extra support (usually from a job coach) to secure employment and learn what's expected of him on the job. The job coach provides initial on-the-job support and then gradually begins to fade out of the picture as the person gains proficiency and becomes more comfortable in the work environment. The job coach might also negotiate the terms of the position with the employer, and be available for follow-up or to assist with problem solving for a period of time. Supported employment has made it possible for many people with developmental disabilities to enter the workforce who might not have been able to compete for a job in the usual way.

Often supported employment is provided through a specialized employment service, but not everyone goes this route and indeed if we consider how most of us found our first job, it probably wasn't through an employment service. More likely, it was through word of mouth or by connecting with people and places in our local community, and maybe finding creative ways to match our skills and interests with possible revenue generating activities. In fact, we've had some success with this approach in our agency. Take Ted, for example:

We started providing support to Ted when he left the institution at age 32. He had never had a job, never went to school, and had spent most of his life on a locked ward with 60 other people with severe disabilities. We knew that Ted enjoyed walking, he liked being outdoors, and he liked going to new places but sometimes only for a few minutes and then he'd want to move on to the next thing. So these were the interests we built on.

Ted quickly became familiar with his new neighbourhood by walking in it several times a day with his support staff. We wanted to find ways for Ted to connect with people in his community and came up with the idea of offering to collect recyclable office paper from local businesses. The City of Vancouver wasn't collecting recycling from businesses as it was for private homes, so each business owner was responsible for disposing of their own recycling or paying for it to be removed. So there was a need for this service, and in fact we met several business owners who were willing to pay Ted to do this for them. At first, the staff did most of the work, but over time as Ted got to know the merchants and became familiar with the routine, he started doing more of the steps. He went from standing behind his staff watching them collect the paper and load it into his pull cart, to standing next to them and receiving armloads of paper to place in the cart, to finally – after many months – completing most of the steps independently, with staff standing back while Ted interacted with the merchants, who looked forward to his visits and valued his services. Over the years, Ted expanded his route, made many new connections, and became known as a contributing member of his community.

Ted's story is an example of *customized employment*, which means creating employment opportunities by matching a person's skills with an employer's needs, as opposed to filling a pre-defined position or responding to an advertisement for employment. With customized employment, we identify the person's unique skill sets and then find a need that an employer might have that could be met by the person's skills. Where traditional job search strategies involve assessing the person's performance against a set of criteria, customized employment emphasizes the process of *discovery,* which involves learning about the person's life experiences, skills and interests in order to achieve the best possible job match. It's a creative approach to job development that expands the notion of work and makes it possible to imagine anyone who wants to work, working. Customized employment challenges us to see each person's unique abilities and figure out how they might put their skills to use and earn an income.

Customized employment starts with identifying the person's areas of interest, skills, preferred environments – outdoors / indoors, fast paced / slower paced – and then matching these with a need that an employer has, or might have. Carving off a portion of an existing job is one way to go about it. For instance, Keith might have an affinity for breaking down cardboard boxes. This could be something an employer is willing to pay someone to do on an occasional or part-time basis, say in a factory or warehouse. Breaking down boxes might not be the responsibility of any one employee, but rather something that everyone is expected to do as needed; so if Keith offers to come in once a week for a couple of hours just to break down cardboard boxes, it might be a welcome contribution that the employer would be willing to pay for.

Self-employment and micro businesses are another approach to customized employment, like the woman we know who makes bath products and sells them at craft fairs. In other examples, people have started their own janitorial business, vending machine business, copy service, cleaning business, consulting and public speaking services.

"Customized employment is a flexible process designed to personalize the employment relationship between a job candidate and an employer in a way that meets the needs of both. It is based on an individualized match between the strengths, conditions, and interests of a job candidate and the identified business needs of an employer. Customized Employment utilizes an individualized approach to employment planning and job development – one person at a time…one employer at a time." (U.S. Department of Labor)

"Social role valorization implies that in order for people to fill and maintain valued roles, they will need *both* a positive social image and personal competencies, and the more they are devalued the more they need these.... The more competencies a person is seen to possess, and the more valued these competencies are, the better an image the person will have in the eyes of observers." (Thomas & Wolfensberger, 1999)

Being physically present in community, having valued roles as friends, neighbours, workers, homeowners / tenants, and being empowered to direct one's own life to the greatest extent possible will go far toward helping people realize their vision of a good life. But it doesn't end there. Each of the roles a person might occupy brings with it role expectancies, tasks and functions that are associated with the role. Being recognized as legitimately occupying a role means fulfilling some or all of the expectancies of the role. Simply claiming that someone is a member of a sports team, or a neighbour, or a customer – whatever the role might be – without supporting the person to learn the role will cause others to view them as being in a kind of token role, but not the real deal. Being a member of a sports team involves attending practices, learning the drills, demonstrating sportsmanship, etc. Being a good neighbour brings with it the expectation that you'll get along with your fellow neighbours, take care of your property, be a positive presence in the neighbourhood, and so on. The more role expectancies people fulfill, the greater their claim to the role and the more others will recognize them as authentically occupying the role.

Supporting people to develop their potential, to learn new skills and increase their independence, is a core value of most human service organizations, but there's rarely much attention paid to equipping staff with the skills to carry out this mandate. In the preceding sections I've provided an overview of some of the history of our field and looked at some of the developments that have prompted a rethinking of old assumptions. In this section I'll talk more specifically about some support strategies that can be useful in helping people to build their competencies and maximize their opportunities for personal growth and development.

What Makes a Good Activity?

Building personal competencies starts with choosing the right activities or skills to focus on. Given the many different ways people might need support, the many competing demands on staff time, and the limited resources we have available to us, it's important that we think critically about where we focus our time and energy. All other things being equal, some of the criteria to consider when choosing one activity over another are:

- The activity aligns with the person's stated goals;

- The activity is typical for others of the same age or from the same culture;

- The activity takes place in an inclusive (not segregated) setting;

- The activity uses generic transportation (walking, transit);

- The activity increases the person's social network;

- The activity can be performed with a variety of people (not dependent on one staff person);

- The activity allows the person to spend time with preferred others;

- The activity allows for active as opposed to passive participation;

- The activity incorporates natural choice points;

- The activity allows the person to contribute to a relationship (reciprocity);

- The activity allows the person to perform a valued social role;

- The activity has the potential for reduced staff involvement over time;

- The activity provides enough of a challenge, or new learning, to sustain the person's interest and motivation;

- The activity occurs with enough frequency to maintain the person's learning over time;

- The activity can be performed in a variety of locations (not dependent on one environment).

As an example, let's say Tom has an interest in classical music. His support worker might take Tom to the Symphony once a month as an activity that supports Tom's interest, and this would satisfy some of the criteria listed above – it's inclusive, it's typical for people Tom's age, it could incorporate some natural choice points (whether to attend an evening performance or a matinee, what to wear, what bus route to take to get there) – but maybe we could take it a step further and find ways for Tom to connect with others who share his interest, or expand upon this activity to build more valued roles around it. Maybe Tom could invite someone else along to the Symphony with him, instead of just going with his support worker. Or he could look into volunteer opportunities at the Symphony, and meet other people who share his love of classical music while also making a valued contribution.

Go Natural!

Too often, we defer to the service system as a first response to meeting people's needs, and generic options as a last resort, if at all. What would happen if we turned this around, and looked to generic, or natural, options as a first response?

Natural environment

The natural environment is wherever you or I would perform a given activity. It's the real world, the real setting, as opposed to an artificial one. An office is the natural environment for learning reception skills; it's not the natural environment for doing arts and crafts. Many service providers have activity space attached to their offices where people with disabilities take part in group activities that are not typical of the activities other people do in offices, like we had in our old drop-in centre. If people are interested in crafting, we should be looking for opportunities for them to do arts and crafts in the community, with others who share their interest, and in places where this activity typically occurs, such as a hobby club or community centre class.

Natural support

Natural support refers to the people and resources that are already in the natural environment, the ones you or I would access. The information desk is a natural support available to anyone at the mall. If you or I need help finding something at the mall, this is where we go to get our questions answered. We don't have support workers beside us anticipating our every need and answering all our questions. Good facilitation involves steering people toward natural supports whenever possible. The old adage *"give a man a fish and you feed him for a day; teach a man to fish and you feed him for a lifetime"* comes to mind here. Natural supports are all around us, we just need to pay attention – and then get out of the way so they can step in. Take Jim, for example. Jim knows that a "blue bill" ($5.00) is enough for a pack of cigarettes, but that's about the extent of his numeracy skills. However, Jim manages his own finances, with help from natural supports. He knows all the tellers at his bank, which he frequents several times a week. They assist him to fill out a withdrawal slip and, assuming he has money in his account, give him a cash withdrawal. If his account is empty, they tell him he'll have to come back in a few days after his next cheque comes through. If they can see his account is running low, they'll suggest he take out $5 that day instead of $10, to tide him over until his next cheque.

Jim is also a frequent customer at a number of local restaurants and coffee shops where he is on a first name basis with the staff and proprietors. In fact, they will even extend him credit when he doesn't have enough to cover his bill. They know he'll be back next week when his cheque clears, and he can always be counted on to repay his debts.

The staff at the bank and the coffee shops see Jim first and foremost as a valued customer, not as someone with a disability. They don't expect Jim to bring a support worker with him to help him fill out forms at the bank or settle his accounts at the restaurant, that's their job. They're the natural supports in these environments.

Natural cues

Natural cues are the cues you or I respond to in a given situation. The walk signal is our cue to cross the street. An overflowing garbage can is our cue to take out the trash. Wherever possible we should be helping people to recognize and respond to natural cues, instead of teaching them to wait for a prompt or permission from a support worker. Natural cues can include self-cueing strategies, like writing appointments in a day timer or making "to do" lists. Teaching someone to use a day timer is preferable to having them rely on staff to keep track of all their appointments.

Natural reinforcement

Natural reinforcement is – you guessed it – the reinforcement you or I would receive in a given situation or for performing a given task. The natural reinforcement for going to work each day is that we get paid. The natural reinforcement for doing our laundry is having clean clothes to wear the next day. Giving someone a gold star for doing their laundry is artificial reinforcement. It's not something that occurs naturally in community. Having your favourite outfit clean and ready to wear out for dinner with friends would be natural reinforcement for doing one's laundry. If artificial reinforcement is used, it should always be paired with natural reinforcement and faded as soon as possible. If the person's only motivation for completing a task is to obtain the artificial reinforcement, then we might want to consider finding another activity that's more intrinsically rewarding.

Natural consequence

A natural consequence is the response or outcome you or I would expect for the choices we make. The natural consequence for not showing up at work is we don't get paid. The natural consequence for making too much noise in the library is we get asked to leave. You and I don't lose our television privileges if we misbehave – that would be an artificial consequence. Effective support involves helping people to understand the natural consequences of their choices.

Fading Staff Support

People with developmental disabilities need the same opportunities as anyone else to learn about and practice problem-solving, and to do so requires us to get out of the way. It's much harder to remove support once people come to depend on it than it is to add more support if people really need it. A bit of struggle or uncertainty isn't a bad thing (remember the *dignity of risk*). There's nothing like those "aha" moments in life when we're unsure what to do next and we figure it out. The process of problem-solving is valuable learning that equips people to deal with the next inevitable challenge life sends their way.

If people are pursuing activities that align with their goals and vision of a good life that they've identified through a process of thoughtful, person-centred planning...then the stage has been set for us to begin to step back. Sometimes we see people being led through activities by their staff, passively participating rather than leading. The person might be connecting with people on a superficial level (*"hey Ken – nice to see you!"*), but the staff serve as a kind of protective shield between the person and other community members. Ken might go grocery shopping at the same store, every week, and months or years later still be following his staff through the store, with the staff person taking the lead and Ken acting in the role of helper. Ken's independence might increase incrementally through sheer repetition of the activity ("*Ken put the all the groceries on the check-out counter by himself today!*") but really, what we're teaching is a kind of learned helplessness. Instead, we should see Ken as the person in charge, and his staff as the helpers. Ken might need a lot of help to begin with, and we might need to slow down and allow more time to get through the activity initially, but as the balance of power starts to shift and Ken's confidence increases, so too will his competence.

Sometimes we just need to get out of the way, like we did with our friend Paul. Paul and his staff had been going to the same coffee shop, every Wednesday morning, for many months. The staff person would go with Paul to the counter, order their drinks, and then help Paul add cream and sugar to his coffee at the side counter. Paul was confident in this activity and had the skills to do each step on his own, but he sometimes spilled a bit of cream or sugar, and he tended to move quite slowly, so his staff preferred to do some of these steps for him so Paul wouldn't get in the way of the other customers or make a mess. He felt this would help to present Paul in a more positive light. One day, Paul's support worker decided to see what would happen if he got out of the way. Instead of going with Paul to the side counter where the cream and sugar were kept, he told Paul he'd meet him over at the table, and left Paul to fix his own coffee. Paul carefully took his coffee to the condiment counter, and added the cream and sugar to his coffee. Another customer, recognizing Paul as one of the regulars, said hello to him and asked how his day was going. They chatted briefly while Paul took his time stirring his coffee. Other customers walked around him to get what they needed, not the least bit concerned that Paul was taking longer than some to get his coffee ready.

Paul completed the task on his own, without spilling anything. And even if had spilled something, he wouldn't be the first person to spill some cream or sugar at the condiment counter. The staff at the coffee shop would have come over and cleaned it up, or someone next to Paul would have helped him wipe up the spill, just as any of us would offer to help someone in a similar situation. That's how it works in community. We help each other wipe up spills. Unfortunately, the human service system sometimes overrides these kinds of ordinary responses by defaulting to paid supporters. Our services sometimes have the unintended effect of pushing ordinary people out of the way, of *disabling* the community, so to speak.

"Human service professionals with special expertise, techniques, and technology push out the problem-solving knowledge and action of friend, neighbor, citizen, and association. As the power of profession and service system ascends, the legitimacy, authority, and capacity of citizens and community descend. The *citizen* retreats. The *client* advances. The power of community action weakens. The authority of the service system strengthens. And as human service tools prevail, the tools of citizenship, association, and community rust. Their uses are even forgotten. Many local people come to believe that the service tool is the only tool, and that their task as good citizens is to support taxes and charities for more services. The consequence of this professional persuasion is devastating for those labeled people whose primary "need" is to be incorporated in community life and empowered through citizenship." (McKnight, 1995)

Think "community first"

Remember Wolfensberger's principle of the *culturally valued analogue* – where would people typically go to pursue an area of interest or learn a new skill? Communities are full of groups for just about any area of interest, and people who want to share their interests with others. Musicians want to spend time with other musicians. Dog lovers enjoy meeting other people who are interested in dogs. There's a multitude of ways in which people connect over shared interests in community, including formal groups like hobby clubs, continuing education classes, sports and recreation groups, service clubs, and community organizations, and informally, such as dog-walking with a friend or visiting the local off-leash park to meet other dog lovers.

Julie might want to learn how to knit. It could be that she has a support worker who also likes knitting and so they decide to start knitting together in the evenings. While they might have a lovely time knitting together, if this is the only opportunity Julie has to knit, and her pursuit of this activity hinges on one staff member, what happens when that person leaves?

Along with knitting at home with her support worker, we would want to ensure that Julie has other avenues for pursuing her interest in knitting, so it can be sustained over time and so she can firmly establish herself in the role of knitter. How do other knitters learn their craft and share their love of knitting? Some ideas might be:

- Talk to Julie's family and friends – see if someone in her network also enjoys knitting;

- Sign up for a knitting class;

- Join a knitting club or knitting meetup group;

- Visit craft fairs and meet other knitters;

- Mentor someone else who wants to learn to knit – learn together and support each other

Staff are not going to be experts at all of the things people might want to learn. Nor is it beneficial for people to rely on staff as the answer to all of their learning needs. If Brian wants to learn about gardening, maybe Brian's dad, or the retired couple next door, might like to help him plant a vegetable garden. Even if Brian's support worker happens to be an expert gardener, if she takes on the task of teaching Brian about gardening, and if she's the only person who shares this part of Brian's life with him, this isn't going to expand Brian's network or provide the opportunities for reciprocity that would come from involving someone else in this activity. Brian's neighbours could help him pick out perennials, and in return Brian could mow their lawn. This would help to establish Brian in the role of good neighbour, which in turn enhances his reputation in the community. Then the support worker's role becomes one of facilitating Brian's relationship with his neighbours and cultivating opportunities to expand upon it.

Instructional approaches

"A lack of learning in any particular situation should first be interpreted as a result of inappropriate or insufficient use of teaching strategies, rather than inability on the part of the learner." (Gold, 1980)

The adult service system evolved alongside the special education system, following the old continuum of services model which emphasized teaching readiness skills, like sorting coins as a precursor to someday learning about budgeting and money management. The practice of congregating people according to their perceived level of functioning was common in adult services, as it was in the school system. Lou Brown, Marc Gold and others saw that this practice was not in keeping with the principles of Normalization and Social Role Valorization. Segregation kept people with developmental disabilities out of community and assigned them to devalued roles with little or no opportunity to move into more valued social roles. It presumed incompetence.

University of Wisconsin professor Lou Brown was an outspoken advocate for change in both the adult service system and the field of special education. At a time when people with severe disabilities were assumed to be uneducable and destined for institutionalization or, at best, non-vocational adult settings, he believed that everyone could live in the community and everyone was capable of making a valuable contribution. *"If you can move one finger, or move your head to one side and push a switch, there's a job for you,"* he would say. He was critical of programs that focused on teaching non-functional tasks, that is, tasks that could only be performed in an artificial setting or that served no useful purpose. Instead, he emphasized teaching *functional skills*, or skills that had practical application in the real world, and not wasting people's time on tasks that had no application outside of a segregated or artificial environment. He proposed the *criterion of ultimate functioning* as a framework for deciding which activities to engage in and which skills to focus on teaching those with severe disabilities:

"If severely handicapped adult citizens are to function effectively in heterogeneous community environments, both handicapped and nonhandicapped citizens will require longitudinal and comprehensive exposure to one another. Such exposure will enhance the probability that the skills, attitudes and values so necessary for tolerance, understanding and absorption will be realized.

"The criterion of ultimate functioning refers to the ever changing, expanding, localized and personalized cluster of factors that each person must possess in order to function as productively and independently as possible in socially, vocationally and domestically integrated adult community environments. Since severely handicapped citizens will ultimately function in settings which contain less handicapped and nonhandicapped citizens, the majority of the developmental environments to which most severely handicapped citizens are now exposed will require substantial changes. Longitudinal segregation, whether manifested in residential institutions or self contained schools, homes or classes will not culminate in the realization of the criterion of ultimate functioning." (Brown, Nietupski & Hamre Nietupski, 1976).

Applying the criterion of ultimate functioning, rather than criteria related solely to the current or immediate environment the person might find himself in, requires a vision of what the person's future could look like and the types of environments he will ultimately be living and working in. In other words, it starts with good person-centred planning. Having a sense of the person's hopes and dreams for the future should inform the selection of activities and learning objectives we set with the person here and now. So if Kyle hopes someday to be working in an office, then teaching him to sort office supplies in a real office would be consistent with the criterion of ultimate functioning. It would help prepare him to function in the environment he hopes someday to be working in. Filling Kyle's day with leisure activities or tasks that aren't related to working in an office would be less beneficial.

Partial participation

Often, a person is able to complete part of a task on his own, but not the whole task. The idea of partial participation is that people should be able to participate in all of the tasks of daily living, to the best of their ability, and not be denied opportunities because they can't do all the steps on their own. Partial participation assumes that everyone can learn, and that participating in an activity partially is better than not participating at all. For example, John might not (yet) be able to cook an entire meal for himself, but participating partially is better than sitting in another room watching t.v. while his staff make dinner.

There are several ways to facilitate partial participation:

1.   *Modify the activity*

        Could the activity be modified to allow the person to complete more of the steps on his own? For example, we might prepare meals in batches and store individual portions in the freezer that John could heat up in the microwave a few nights a week, instead of expecting him to make every meal from scratch. If peeling and cutting up fresh vegetables poses a challenge, then perhaps John could learn to heat up frozen vegetables instead.

2.   *Environmental adaptations*

        From the high tech (voice activation software) to low tech (on / off switch) to no tech (coloured stickers), the possibilities for adapting an activity or environment are endless. For example, if John has difficulty using the knobs on the stove, we could replace them with knobs that are easier for him to use.

3.   *Targeted assistance*

> If the person needs assistance, then that assistance should be focused on the parts of the activity he's not able to do by himself. For example, even with modifications or adaptations, John still might only be able to complete 50% of the task of making dinner. However, with practice and perhaps some targeted instruction on incrementally more steps, over time John could be doing 60% of the meal preparation, then 70%, and so on.

There are as many ways to teach as there are individual learning styles. Some people enjoy learning through lecture or demonstration, by watching and observing; others are more experiential and learn by doing; others like to figure things out on their own through trial and error. Chances are most of us use a combination of these approaches, depending on the situation and what it is we want to learn. We might take swimming lessons from a certified swimming instructor to learn the proper techniques to keep us safe in the water, but ask a family member or friend to show us the bus route for getting to the pool, or look up the directions ourselves online.

One way to think about types of instruction is to think in terms of a continuum of approaches, from direct instruction to indirect instruction, or teacher-centred to learner-centred.

Direct instruction

Direct instruction refers to a set of approaches that focus on teaching a particular set of skills or sequence of steps, for example learning to swim, drive a car, or operate an appliance. With direct instruction, the goal is to help the learner gain mastery and then be able to perform the task independently, or with less support over time. Even for tasks that involve discrete or prescribed steps (for example, learning how to operate a dishwasher), there are any number of different ways one might go about teaching the task. *Systematic instruction*, which comes out of Marc Gold's "Try another Way" philosophy, puts the onus on the instructor to find an approach that suits the individual's learning needs, instead of expecting all learners to respond to one teaching method. The strategies described below are just a few examples of direct instructional strategies, but it's by no means an exhaustive list. Be creative! And be open to changing your approach if it isn't working. To paraphrase Marc Gold, if at first you don't succeed, *"try another way."*

Hierarchy of Prompts

Direct instruction requires careful attention to the way we provide assistance, and perhaps most especially to *prompting*. Prompts can be thought of as information or directions we provide above and beyond the natural cues that you or I would respond to in the same situation. There's a whole hierarchy of prompts, ranging from most directive to least directive:

Physical prompts

- Full physical prompt – eg. hand-over-hand assistance to get lunch out of the fridge
- Partial physical prompt – eg. shoulder tap to direct the person to the fridge

Verbal prompts

- Direct verbal prompt – eg. "get your lunch out of the fridge"
- Indirect verbal prompt – eg. "are you getting hungry?"

Visual prompts

- eg. getting the person's lunch bag out of the fridge and holding it up for him to see

Demonstration prompts, or modeling

- eg. the support person gets her own lunch, demonstrating to the person what's expected

Object prompts, or positioning

- eg. putting a plate on the counter next to the person, as a cue to get his lunch

Gestural prompts

- eg. pointing to the fridge

Self prompts

- eg. the person's watch is pre-set to start beeping at noon

Paying attention to prompting can help to set things up for success. Too much prompting, and the person will become reliant on our prompts; too little prompting, and the person might feel overwhelmed or not know what to do. Everyone wants to experience the satisfaction and sense of accomplishment that comes from completing a task on their own. One of the most common mistakes we see staff making is over-prompting people. It's usually done out of good intentions – we all want to be helpful – but our good intentions can further disable people by causing them to doubt their own instincts and become over-reliant on our artificial cues (*"I think it's time to eat, but my staff haven't told me to get my lunch yet, so I'd better wait"*). *Prompt dependence* occurs when people know what to do, but wait for someone to tell them instead of taking the initiative themselves. Prompt dependence makes it very difficult to fade our support. We want people to have the confidence to decide for themselves when it's time to initiate an activity or take the next step. To that end, whenever we use prompts, we should be conscious of reducing them as soon as possible, and encouraging people to respond to natural cues.

Task analysis

A task analysis is a useful tool for taking an objective look at the activity or skill the person wants to learn. It involves breaking a task into separate steps, where the completion of each step in the sequence is the natural cue to initiate the next step. For example, a task analysis for making coffee might look like this:

1.   *Place coffee filter into filter basket*

2.   *Measure 100 ml. ground coffee into filter*

3.   *Fill carafe with water to 12 cup line*

4.   *Pour water into coffee maker*

5.   *Turn switch to "on"*

If more than one person is teaching the task, a task analysis helps to ensure that everyone is following the same steps. It's especially useful for simple, repetitive tasks where the person has frequent opportunities for practice.

Discrepancy Analysis

A discrepancy analysis is simply looking at the gaps between what the person is able to do without our assistance, and what steps they need help with. It's a baseline, or starting point, for determining where we need to focus our support. In our coffee example, let's say Sarah can place the filter in the basket, measure the coffee, and pour the water into the machine, but she needs hand-over-hand assistance to measure the water and a verbal prompt to turn the switch on.

Measuring the water and turning on the switch are the *discrepant* steps, or the ones Sarah needs help with. Remember, we don't want to add unnecessary prompts, so if Sarah is able to do some steps independently, let her! For the steps she isn't yet able to do, we may decide to adapt the task to make it easier – for example, drawing a red line on the carafe to indicate how far to fill it – or begin systematically fading our prompts each time Sarah completes the task (fading from a direct to an indirect verbal prompt, to a gestural prompt, etc.).

Shaping

Margaret lived in an institution for the first 30 years of her life. Because Margaret was blind and somewhat unsteady on her feet, she was discouraged from moving about the ward. Margaret was small in stature, and so the staff on the ward would sometimes carry her from one place to another. When she wasn't being carried, she would sit in an armchair in the corner of the day room or lie in her bed.

As we were setting up Margaret's home in the community, we wanted to strike a balance between her need for safety and opportunities for her to begin to explore her surroundings and increase her independent mobility. We decided that teaching Margaret to walk from her bedroom to the bathroom would be a good place to start, using a *shaping* approach to incrementally increase the distance she would walk unaided by staff. We attached a strip of fuzzy fabric to the wall, running from her bedroom to the bathroom (a distance of about 12 feet), at Margaret's waist level, the idea being that she would feel her way along the wall to the bathroom. We put masking tape markers at six inch increments on the wall above the fuzzy strip. Initially, we would walk next to Margaret the whole way, manually guiding her hand along the wall so she could feel the fabric, all the way to the final destination – a warm bath, which she could hear running as she made her way down the hall. Once she got comfortable with the routine, we removed the first masking tape marker (6 inches from the end of the fuzzy strip, and within arm's length of the bathtub). The next day we escorted Margaret to that point, and then placed her hand on the side of the tub so she could take the last step on her own. The next day, we removed the second masking tape marker, and Margaret walked the final 12 inches of the way by herself, and so on, until she was walking the whole distance by herself. Within about a month, Margaret was getting out of bed and walking to the bathroom independently – further than she'd ever walked on her own.

The instructional strategy we used to teach Margaret to walk to the bathroom is called *shaping*. Shaping involves gradually increasing the person's independence through repetition of the task, or through successive approximations to the end result.

Chaining

Chaining refers to linking one step in a sequence to the next. For example, let's say you're teaching Laura to make a bag lunch to take to work the next day. The steps might be as follows:

> 1.   *Fill water bottle and place in lunch bag;*
>
> 2.   *Place cookies in lunch bag;*
>
> 3.   *Make a sandwich;*
>
> 4.   *Place sandwich in lunch bag;*
>
> 5.   *Place lunch bag in fridge*

There are a couple of different ways to use chaining as an instructional strategy:

> *Forward chaining:*   With forward chaining, you would start with the first step, and teach Laura to fill her water bottle and place it in her lunch bag. You would work on this step until she perfected it, and then move on to teaching the next step in the task. The drawback with forward chaining is that it can take a long time to get around to teaching the final step, and so the satisfaction of completing the task might be quite

delayed. Laura might learn to put the water bottle and cookies in her lunch bag, but get stuck on the step of making a sandwich, or take a longer time to work through that step. So from Laura's perspective, she's learning to start the task and get part way through it, but maybe never getting to complete it.

Reverse chaining: With reverse chaining, you start by teaching the last step in the sequence, so in our lunch-making example the staff would get everything done ahead of time – all the items prepared and put into the lunch bag – and then bring Laura in to do the last step of placing the lunch bag in the fridge. So right away, Laura gets to see the end result and experience the completion of the task. Then you'd work backwards, adding the second to last step, then the third to last step, and so on, back to the beginning, until eventually Laura is completing the whole task on her own.

Compensatory strategies

If we find we're unable to reduce our prompts because John simply doesn't remember what to do next, we might try writing down the instructions on a cue card that he can refer to, or audiotaped instructions, or teaching him to use an electronic organizer. These are examples of using compensatory strategies, or strategies that help to compensate for a loss of function or an inability to complete a task in the usual way. Compensatory strategies are often used by people with brain injuries who must learn new ways of doing things in order to cope with memory loss, difficulty with visual or auditory processing, or other effects of their injury. If someone gets frustrated easily, a compensatory strategy to support her independence might be to allow the person more time to complete complex tasks, or building in extra breaks. If the person has trouble remembering where she's supposed to be throughout the day, she could carry a datebook with her schedule clearly written out and important information at her fingertips.

Baseline

A baseline is a snapshot of a person's proficiency with a task at a particular point in time. A task analysis is one way to do a baseline, by walking through the steps of the task and observing which parts the person can do on his own, which parts he needs prompting with, and which parts might require an adaptation or modification. A baseline gives you a starting point. It also gives you something to refer back to, so you can more accurately track the person's progress (or even better, he can track it himself) and celebrate successes. Let's say John wants to learn how to heat up a can of soup by himself. Heating up a can of soup independently might not seem like cause for celebration, but if John was only able to stir the soup with hand-over-hand assistance two months ago, completing the whole task on his own now is a major accomplishment. Given the high turnover in our field, a baseline and some form of reliable documentation of the person's progress gives new people coming into the person's life valuable perspective.

Baseline is a term we often associate with behavioural support programs, as in taking a baseline of the frequency and duration of a target behaviour. Systematic instruction, or direct instruction, comes out of the field of applied behavioural analysis, and shares with it a focus on discrete, observable actions and the manipulation of environmental variables to promote learning of a new skill or behaviour. There are tasks that lend themselves to this kind of approach, but not all learning happens in a systematic, orderly fashion. Likewise, not all learners take to the formality of systematic instruction. The next section will describe some indirect instructional approaches.

Indirect instruction

Indirect instruction refers to approaches that are more learner-directed, where the person takes a more active role in his own learning. Experiential learning, or learning from experience, is a common example, and indeed much of our learning as adults happens this way, like learning how to cook. Most of us acquired some basic cooking skills by helping out in the kitchen as children, and then advanced to learning new recipes, reading cookbooks, possibly taking a cooking class, and a lot of trial and error.

Experiments, observation, interviews, group discussion, case studies, independent research (doing internet searches, subscribing to magazines or online discussion boards) and journaling are all examples of indirect learning. Some approaches that can be applied to a variety of learning situations for people with developmental disabilities include:

Co-learning

Co-learning occurs when two people learn something together, as opposed to one person teaching the other. Instead of thinking in terms of what staff can teach the person with a disability, it can be more empowering to frame the experience as co-learning. For example, James and his support worker could take a cooking class together, or take out cookbooks from the library and learn a new recipe together. This approach can help to level the playing field and create natural opportunities for the person to take the lead, as opposed to assuming that staff have all the answers and the person is on the receiving end of their teaching. So if James wants to learn how to make lasagne, instead of the staff saying *"I know how to make lasagne – let me show you,"* they could say, *"Let's look at some recipes and you can pick the one you like – we'll figure it out together."* This way, James isn't just learning how to make lasagne, he's learning how to do research, he's practicing choice-making, and he's taking a leadership role in his own learning.

Increase wait time

Sometimes the best way to tell if it's time to fade our support is to step back, and wait. Give the person a few seconds, or minutes even, to figure out what to do next. Sometimes people are so used to having staff take the lead, they'll wait for us to make the first move, even when they know what's supposed to happen next. If Sarah is waiting for you to prompt her to turn on the coffee maker, see what happens if you say nothing, or if you simply walk away.

A study by educator Mary Budd Rowe looked on the wait time, or pauses, in interactions between students and teachers, and found that increased wait time resulted in better quality responses, increased student confidence, and an increase in the number of unsolicited (ie. unprompted) responses:

> "When teachers ask questions of students, they typically wait 1 second or less for the students to start a reply; after the student stops speaking they begin their reaction or proffer the next question in less than 1 second. If teachers can increase the average length of the pauses...there are pronounced changes in student use of language and logic as well as in student and teacher attitudes and expectations." (Rowe, 1986).

Transitions are a good time to practice increasing wait time between prompts, for example ending an activity (finishing lunch and deciding what to do next) or leaving a situation or environment (leaving home in the morning). We are creatures of habit, we all have our routines. When I finish dinner, I pick up my plate and take it to the sink, then I pack up any leftovers and put them in the fridge, then I clear the table, and so on. Chances are, in these routine activities of daily living, people know what to do next. They don't need us to tell them all the steps. Try stepping back, and see what happens if you don't prompt Sarah through all the steps of getting ready to leave the house in the morning. Or try eliminating one prompt at a time, to get her used to the idea. Or just slow it down. Wait a little longer between instructions. When you come to a natural transition point in an activity, wait before giving an instruction – the pause will be a natural cue that something is supposed to happen and an opportunity for the person to problem solve.

Rehearsal

Rehearsing the steps ahead of time can minimize the prompting you'll need to provide during the activity. It also reduces the need for correcting the person after the fact if she gets it wrong. Nobody likes being corrected. Role playing, practicing a scripted interaction, or talking through a scenario are ways we can clarify the expectations in advance and make sure people have the information and tools they'll need to be successful. Going into a new situation, or meeting new people, can be stressful for anyone. Talking about what to expect ahead of time, rehearsing how you might enter the room, where you'll sit, how you'll introduce yourself, can help to alleviate some of the stress. It can also help to give the person a role, or something to contribute. For example, Kim could bring a bottle of wine to her friend's barbecue, so when she walks in she'll have something to give her host. This will help to reinforce Kim's role as a guest, and will also create an opportunity for a positive interaction with her host. If walking into a room full of people makes Kim anxious, think of something she might focus on: *"Bring your pictures from Whistler and you can show them to Margie – she went to Whistler last summer."* This will give Kim something to look forward to when she arrives, instead of worrying about who might be there, what they might expect from her, etc.

Debrief

Equally beneficial to rehearsing something ahead of time is debriefing after the fact. When you get home from the event, talk to Kim about how it went – what worked, what didn't work, what might she do differently next time?

Debriefing should be constructive, and positive. Any feedback should focus on what the person did well, and ideas for things to try next time, eg. *"Next time we'll get there a few minutes early so you'll have more time to get settled,"* instead of *"Next time don't be so impatient."* It's an opportunity for positive reinforcement and for celebrating success, as in *"Margie sure enjoyed looking at your pictures,"* or *"You were hoping to talk to a few people, but you talked to everyone! You seemed very comfortable – how did you feel?"*

Debriefing is a reflective practice, where the goal is to gain insights that can help guide future learning. It's something many of us do intuitively, for example when we leave work at the end of the day we reflect on whether we accomplished what we set out to that day. We can build in debriefing to any activity, even if it's just asking simple questions afterwards like, *"how was that for you?"* or *"what did you like about that activity?"* Sometimes people aren't used to being asked for their opinion, or being expected to think critically about what they've accomplished, what they liked and didn't like about an activity – their experience might be that others decide things for them, or that their opinion doesn't matter. Debriefing is a way to teach critical thinking and promote a sense of empowerment.

Behavioural support

Some of the people we know are described as having difficult or challenging behaviour. They might have professional supports (psychologists, behavioural therapists, mental health workers) who work with the team to establish protocols for dealing with their behaviour. There are strict guidelines for behaviour management that generally require any behavioural programs to be signed off and overseen by someone with special training in behavioural support.

There's a whole range of behavioural interventions, ranging from less restrictive, like positive reinforcement (eg. ice-cream as a reward for getting through the day with no episodes of aggression) and token economies (eg. earning stickers at set intervals throughout the day and cashing them in for a reward), to more restrictive, such as negative reinforcement (removal of positive reinforcement, eg. no ice-cream if the person misbehaves) or punishment (addition of a negative consequence, eg. being sent to bed early). In institutions, people who acted out or caused a disturbance were subdued through the use of chemical or physical restraints, or secluded in time-out rooms. Such practices are prohibited in community settings, unless approved in writing by a physician, and even then are considered an option of last resort. In some jurisdictions, they are not allowed at all.

The behavioural approach comes out of BF Skinner's operant conditioning model for understanding behavior, which was introduced in the 1950s. Skinner believed that behavior was driven by the reinforcement that followed it, which could be positive, negative, or neutral. Behaviors that were positively reinforced would increase in frequency or in their *rate of response,* while those that were negatively reinforced would decrease in frequency. A neutral response would neither increase nor decrease the rate of response. Skinner devised a system for describing and manipulating behavior through what he termed *schedules of reinforcement* (Ferster & Skinner, 1957). While Skinner's work was not focused on people with developmental disabilities, his ideas were widely adopted by the human service system and by the special education system.

Behaviour modification was very popular in the 1970s, and was adopted as a treatment approach in many of the early community living services. By the 1980s, the concept of *positive behavioural support* emerged, which broadened the scope of behaviour modification beyond simply reducing or eliminating problematic behaviour. Positive behavioural support looks at a person's behaviour in its larger context, ie. factors in the environment that might be causing or contributing to the person's behaviour. It seeks to understand the function that the person's behaviour serves, and to teach alternative behaviours that will better serve the person.

Some potential drawbacks of behavioural approaches

A little knowledge can be a dangerous thing

Behavioural strategies require a substantial investment of time and energy, and a commitment on the part of all involved to following through on the program consistently. There's the initial investment of time and expertise to develop a comprehensive behavioural support plan, and then the ongoing work of monitoring and revising the plan, ensuring everyone responsible for implementing the plan is properly trained, tracking progress on the plan, and communicating with all of the various professional supports and team members. Inattention to any of these elements, cutting corners to save time or implementing quick fix solutions, can compromise the integrity of the process. Given the high rate of staff turnover in our field, and the many competing demands on staff time, making sure everyone is adequately trained and kept apprised of changes in the person's behaviour, or changes to the plan, is no small task. If Don's behaviour program depends on him getting a choice of preferred activities in the evening as positive reinforcement for getting through the day without any episodes of aggression, and Don's support worker forgets to offer the reinforcement or gets busy with something else, then our credibility in Don's eyes goes out the window.

The complexity of behavioural programming makes for a high probability of error on the part of those implementing the program. A good behavioural support program will be heavily weighted on the side of proactive strategies (things that can be done to prevent the person's behaviour from escalating) and less so on the reactive side (how we respond when an escalation occurs). This requires a level of rigour that can be hard to sustain, especially with multiple people involved in implementing the program. So for example, making sure Don gets out for a long walk first thing in the morning might be an important proactive strategy to help him expend some energy and reduce the chances of an escalation later in the day; but if the new relief staff hasn't yet been trained in the program, or if it's raining and they decide to postpone the walk, Don's anxiety will increase because the expected routine isn't happening, and by lunch time he might be hitting people or throwing pieces of furniture around.

It's human nature to put things off, to minimize preventive steps and wait for things to escalate before we deal with them. Even if the behaviour program is heavily weighted on the side of prevention, with reactive or restrictive steps meant to be used only if the preventive part doesn't work, there's a high probability that staff won't follow the program with 100% consistency, and the last-resort responses will get resorted to more often than not. So the person might lose out on reinforcement he's entitled to, or be punished for acting out, through no fault of his own.

Behavioural approaches can be disempowering for the person

While the stated goal of behavioural support plans is instructive, ie. teaching the person functional skills or more adaptive behaviour to replace an undesirable behaviour, they often set up a power struggle that detracts from the learning objectives, and that raises a host of ethical questions. Even the use of positive reinforcement – like giving someone a can of pop for doing her laundry – can be interpreted as punitive, in that it makes a preferred item contingent on completing a certain task or performing certain behaviours. You or I are free to get a can of pop if we want one. In fact, it's very difficult to think of reinforcers that are both motivating to the person (and will therefore be effective) and that we can offer contingently, without infringing on the person's rights. What gives us the right to say someone can only have access to a preferred item when she complies with our demands? We're inviting a power struggle when we impose conditions or restrictions on people that you or I wouldn't tolerate ourselves. Power struggles favour the person with the most power, and where behavioural programs are concerned that's usually the staff.

While positive approaches emphasize teaching alternative behaviours, their success is generally measured by the degree to which the target behaviour is reduced, or in other words, the degree to which the person complies with the program and does what we expect her to do. But is compliance really something we want to celebrate? What if the behaviour we consider to be problematic is the person's only way of saying "NO!" Sheila might have found screaming to be an effective way of protecting herself at some point in the past. Eliminating screaming from her repertoire could have the unintended effect of making her more vulnerable to abuse.

Behavioural approaches can further traumatize the person

There's a growing body of research into post traumatic stress disorder (PTSD), a severe anxiety disorder that can result from witnessing or experiencing a traumatic event. Dr. David Pitonyak has studied the impact of trauma on the lives of people with developmental disabilities, who are much more likely than people without disabilities to have experienced trauma in the form of abuse, neglect, separation from family at a young age, or any number of other factors. Statistics show that people with developmental disabilities experience much higher rates of physical and sexual abuse than the general population (Sobsey, 1994, Razza, Tomasulo & Sobsey, 2011). While not everyone who experiences abuse will develop PTSD, it's likely that many of the people we support have experienced trauma at some point in their lives, and some will meet the criteria for PTSD. Some of the symptoms of PTSD include:

- Recurring thoughts or dreams about the traumatic event that are intensely distressing;
- Avoiding activities, places or people that remind the person of the traumatic event;
- Difficulty sleeping;
- Irritability or angry outbursts;
- Hyper vigilance   (DSM – IV, 1994)

In other words, some of the behaviours that might get labeled as challenging or problematic could, in fact, be symptoms of PTSD. Treating these kinds of symptoms as a behaviour problem instead of understanding and addressing the underlying trauma could further traumatize the person. I think back to Walter, the man who was befriended by the grocery store cashier, and how many of his behaviours probably indicated PTSD. We knew that Walter had been kept in seclusion on many occasions during his time in the institution, which probably explained his aversion to enclosed spaces – he ripped his bedroom door off its hinges three times before we got the message and left it off for good. Walter didn't speak, so he couldn't tell us if he was having flashbacks or nightmares, but there's no doubt in my mind that he was. He would sometimes start screaming, for no apparent reason, with a look of terror on his face. Walter carried a collection of small objects with him everywhere – an old tennis ball, a plastic ring, pieces of string – and if he misplaced something he would literally tear the house apart until he found it. He rarely slept, but whenever he did manage to fall asleep, he would wake up in a panic a short time later and begin searching for whatever object he'd invariably dropped on the floor when he dozed off. We later learned from someone who knew him in the institution that the staff used to tie his objects to a fence post out of his reach whenever he was outside on the institution grounds, as a way to keep him from wandering off. Walter would stand at the fence, fixated on his precious objects. Walter's anxiety was off the charts, even though he was taking three times the recommended dosage of anti-anxiety medication for someone his size.

Anyone who has experienced acute anxiety will be familiar with the "fight or flight" response. In times of extreme stress, the part of our brain that deals with complex thought essentially shuts down, and our instinct for self preservation kicks in. Even if there is no actual imminent danger, the body responds as if there is: our heart rate increases, our breathing becomes more rapid, we begin to sweat. Our capacity for rational thought is greatly reduced. Behavioural approaches will have little effect if the person is not able to follow instructions or even comprehend what is being asked of him. He simply might be unable, in that moment, to process information, and our interventions might even cause further trauma.

Reframing challenging behaviour

"People with severe reputations are our teachers if we are wise enough to learn from them. Their behaviour [is] often telling us:

- You are not giving me the help I need

- You are hurting me

- Your ideas may be good but your actions aren't

- You can do better"   (Lovett, 1996)

Behaviour management is premised on the idea that challenging behaviour is a problem within the person, and as such the goal is to eliminate it or replace it with more adaptive or functional behaviours. A different way of thinking about people with so-called challenging behavior is to think of them as people who challenge the system, or to locate the problem in the environment rather than in the person. So instead of approaching the problem from the perspective of *"how do we change the person's behaviour?"* our focus would be, *"how might we change the environment or change our approach to better support the person?"*

Wilma, who lived on the same ward as Walter in the institution, was described to us as being severely self-abusive. Several times a day, she would hit herself in the head, for no apparent reason. Small scars were visible on the sides of her face, and both of her ears were deformed from years of self injury. Shortly after she moved into her new home, the staff noticed that Wilma would hold food in her cheeks for an hour or more after meals, and also after being given her medication, which she took with a spoonful of applesauce. The staff discovered that as the applesauce dissolved, the pills would sit in Wilma's mouth and her behaviour would start to escalate. She was reacting to the unpleasant taste of the pills. Her staff started crushing her pills and mixing them with a bigger serving of applesauce, and Wilma's self injurious behaviour went down dramatically.

Behaviour is not random. When someone acts out or creates a disturbance, there's a reason for it. The biggest mistake we can make is trying to "fix" people's behaviour without understanding it. Most of the time, the cause or underlying function of the behaviour falls into one of three categories:

1. Communication: The person is trying to tell us something

2. Unmet needs: The person has needs that are not being met

3. Environmental factors: Something in the environment is causing the person distress

Remember, everyone communicates. Most of us know how to communicate and get our needs met without causing a disturbance or drawing negative attention to ourselves. We understand social cues, and can adjust our behaviour to suit different situations. We have a repertoire of communication skills that we've developed and refined over a lifetime. However, when we're feeling stressed, our words might not come so easily, or with their usual politeness. Our behaviour might stray from what would be considered socially appropriate. We might become irritable, raise our voices or make threatening gestures. Anyone who has driven in city traffic has seen otherwise mild mannered adults behave badly when another car cuts them off. If the source of our distress persists, or worsens, there will likely be a corresponding escalation in our behaviour.

A person with a developmental disability might have had fewer opportunities to learn social skills. Or they might communicate in ways that aren't readily understood by others. Their choices and movements are sometimes limited by what might seem to them arbitrary rules, designed to keep them safe or maintain order. If I'm feeling restless, I can get up and go outside for a walk. If I weren't allowed to go outside, or if the door was locked and I didn't have the key to open it, my restlessness would escalate to frustration and anger. There would most certainly be a change in my behaviour.

Even people with very sophisticated communication skills will occasionally raise their voice in anger, storm out of a room, slam a door in frustration. People with limited communication abilities have fewer options for expressing themselves. If I'm waiting for my friend to finish working on the computer and come shopping with me, I can ask when she's going to be done, or tell her to hurry up, or decide to go without her. Someone with limited communication might feel the same frustration at having to wait, but won't be able to express it in the same way – and so where I will ask questions, someone with fewer communication skills might yell or throw something. If yelling or throwing something is the only way the person knows how to express frustration, then we can reasonably expect him to resort to these behaviours when he is feeling stressed. It's not random at all, it's actually very predictable.

So a good place to start when looking at challenging behaviour is to ask, *"what is the person trying to say?"*

Looking at behaviour through the lens of communication gives us empathy for the person, who might be trying to communicate in the only way he knows how. It's not an exact science, however. One behaviour might be communicating many different things, and likewise one communication message (*"I'm bored"*) might be conveyed through a variety of different behaviours: the person might rock back and forth, start pacing the floor, make certain kinds of vocalizations. There could be a whole range, or hierarchy of behaviours the person uses to communicate one message. If rocking back and forth doesn't get our attention, the person might start pacing the floor, and if that doesn't work, he might start yelling, and so on.

Hierarchy of behaviour and response

Behaviour often follows a pattern of escalation, starting with the first signs of distress and progressing from there. A really useful exercise to do with the team is to write up the pattern of behaviour we can expect to see if the person is feeling stressed, and the optimal response that supporters can offer at each step. By paying attention to these patterns, we can begin to honour the person's communication more reliably so he doesn't feel the need to escalate. As the person comes to trust that we will respond to his attempts at communication, his sense of predictability and control will increase, which in turn will help to reduce his stress level and lessen the chances of a full blown escalation.

Level 4: "I'm feeling out of control / I'm in a state of panic"		
Level 3: "I'm very upset / angry / scared"		
Level 2: "I'm getting upset / frustrated"		
Level 1: "I'm feeling a bit stressed"		
	Describe what this looks like, ie. the person's behaviour	Describe the optimal response that will be most helpful to the person

People sometimes get a bit irritable when they're tired, or hungry, or if they're feeling sick. Richard might have seasonal allergies, and need relief from his symptoms. Or he might be uncomfortable – too hot or too cold, or his shoes are too tight, or he's bothered by the lighting or noise in the environment. Wilma's self injurious behaviour reduced by about 80% when we started crushing her pills, because she no longer had to sit for hours with an unpleasant taste in her mouth. We've met people with sores on their bodies that no-one has noticed or bothered to treat; people with ingrown toenails or urinary tract infections or abscessed teeth – things that were causing them pain and discomfort, which, not surprisingly, sometimes manifested in angry outbursts, self injury, or acts of aggression. Behaviour management isn't going to cure a toothache.

Satisfying basic needs, like sleep, nutrition, medical and dental care, should be a given. But if we think back to Michael Kendrick's domains of need, a good life is about much more than getting one's basic needs met. Even if the person has all of his physical and physiological needs satisfied, he might have unmet needs in other areas that cause him even greater distress – relationships, for example.

Often when we look at people's history, we'll discover that their behaviour changed following some significant life event, and in particular the disruption of an important relationship – the death of a loved one, separation from their family, loss of friendships upon leaving school or moving to a new city. Typically people enter the service system during times of transition in their lives, for example moving out of the family home for the first time or finishing school and coming into adult services. Maybe the person has been living with older parents or caregivers who now need care themselves, or an elderly parent passes away, forcing a sometimes sudden or unexpected move for the grieving son or daughter. Or there might have been a breakdown in the person's previous living situation due to a divorce, or conflict with other people in the home, prompting a move. Few things in life are more stressful than moving, and when it's coupled with the trauma of losing a loved one or close personal relationships, a change in behaviour is to be expected.

David Pitonyak would say that social isolation and a lack of satisfying personal relationships are the root cause of much of what we label as challenging behaviour, and that addressing unmet relationship needs is what we should focus on, not behavioural change:

"I believe that loneliness is the number one cause of difficult behaviors. It is not the only cause, of course, it is just the most common one. We are relational beings and the absence of meaningful relationships makes us sick. It wears us down to the point where we can't see straight. If you have difficulty believing it, if it seems too "touchy-feely," imagine yourself without the people you love for 30 days. You have no idea where they have gone. Now imagine being without them for sixty days...or ninety...or more. How are you feeling? Are you sleeping well? What is your mood? My bet is that you are falling apart. My bet is that you are spiralling out of control. You want to be logical about all of this, but reason has taken a back seat to longing." (Pitonyak, 2006)

If someone's shoes are too tight, there's a quick fix for that – get some shoes that fit. Addressing a person's need for meaningful relationships might be more challenging. But it could be that it's the most important thing we need to pay attention to, the thing that overrides all other needs. To paraphrase Dr. Pitonyak, get the relationships right and everything else starts to fall into place; get it wrong and nothing else matters.

Environmental factors

"There is no such thing as a behaviour problem. There is only conflict. Conflict presumes equal power." (Kunc & Van der Klift, 2012)

In a workplace, if an employee has a dispute with a co-worker or supervisor, we call it conflict. We refer the two parties to the conflict resolution procedure and, if necessary, we involve a neutral third party to negotiate a resolution. If a person with a developmental disability has a dispute with his support worker or refuses to comply with a request, we call it a behaviour problem. Imagine how different the response might be, how much more empowered the person would feel, if we framed the issue as conflict instead of as a behaviour problem; if instead of seeing John's refusal to take a shower in the morning as non-compliance, we thought of it as assertiveness, or as John making a choice to do something different. Instead of putting our energy into convincing John to have a shower, or coming up with schedules of reinforcement to reward him for showering when we think he should shower, we could seek to understand what he'd rather do instead. Maybe he'd prefer to shower at night. Maybe he'd rather take a bath. Or maybe it's just one staff member who John doesn't like taking direction from, and the solution would be not to have that person asking John to take a shower.

Very often in human services, people are expected to follow routines that someone else has put in place, without having a clear understanding of the rationale for why things are the way they are, or being given the option of establishing routines that make sense for them. If people feel disempowered, or if our expectations make no sense to them, they likely will act out in order to reclaim some of their power.

I remember attending a training session on positive approaches for dealing with challenging behaviour, and the speaker asked us all to imagine what we'd do if he told us our lunch break was being cancelled and we wouldn't be getting anything to eat until the end of the day. Some of us said we'd be annoyed but we'd put up with it; others said they would leave at noon anyway, and miss some of the presentation. Then he asked us to imagine that the doors had been locked and we weren't going to be allowed to leave until he gave us permission. We all agreed this would increase our anxiety and would probably lead us to behave in ways we wouldn't normally behave. Some said they would break down the door and would even resort to violence if necessary to gain control of the situation.

Behavioural outbursts can be seen as an attempt to restore the balance of power. Ironically, the more a person's behaviour begins to escalate, the more restrictions generally get placed on them, or stated differently, the more of their power gets taken away from them. We shouldn't be surprised, then, if the person's behaviour escalates further. It's like applying pressure to a spring – the resistance increases until eventually it snaps.

Sometimes the person's sense of disempowerment stems from a lack of information or understanding about what's expected. For example, John might be in an unfamiliar situation and not know what the expectations are, or what's going to happen next (*How long are we going to be here? When will I get lunch? Where is the bathroom?*). Imagine what it must be like not to know who's going to show up to be with you from one day to the next, or one shift to the next. Imagine if you needed help getting in and out of bed, having a bath, eating your meals – and not knowing when you go to bed at night who's going to be there in the morning to help you. Or imagine that you do know who's going to be there, and it's someone you don't like. A lack of predictability and control will make anyone uneasy, and so we shouldn't be surprised when people push back.

Before getting to any kind of intervention, we should start by looking closely at the circumstances surrounding the person's behaviour, for example:

- *Where* is the behaviour most likely to occur? Where is it least likely to occur?

- *When* is the behaviour most likely to occur? When is it least likely to occur?

- *With whom* is the behaviour most likely to occur? Least likely to occur?

Once we have a clear sense of the context for the behaviour, then we can begin to structure things so as to maximize the time the person spends with preferred others, doing preferred activities, and minimize the time spent with less preferred people, in environments that are more likely to trigger the behaviour.

Supportive approaches

Supportive, or proactive, strategies are the things we can do to help prevent an escalation in the person's behaviour. *Reactive strategies* refer to steps we might take after the fact, in response to an escalation in the person's behaviour. If the person is known to become extremely violent or threatening, even with all of the proactive steps in place to minimize such an occurrence, then a well planned response to deal with a potential escalation is an important part of the person's overall support plan. Specific reactive strategies – that is, strategies for responding to a potentially dangerous situation – would be developed by someone with expertise in this area, and should never be undertaken without proper training and oversight. However, the best emergency response is good prevention. That's where supportive approaches come in.

People who do things that are harmful to themselves or others might need support to figure out other ways of getting their needs met. It would be unethical to stand by and allow someone to injure himself repeatedly without intervening. Similarly, it would be irresponsible to send staff in to support someone who is known to behave in potentially harmful ways without preparing them for how to deal with an escalation. But a person's behaviour should always be considered within the context of an overall support plan, a plan that the person has contributed to, that reflects his lifestyle and preferences, that honours his communication and relationships, and

115

that actively promotes his inclusion in places and activities of his choosing. Behavioural interventions absent this context are likely to be ineffective, and even harmful.

Before looking to behavioural interventions, the prudent course of action would be to spend some time getting to know the person, establishing a foundation of trust from which to begin building a relationship.

Listen deeply

If you or I were behaving oddly, someone – a family member, friend or co-worker – would sit us down and talk about it. They'd ask us what was going on. They'd ask if there was anything they could do to help. They wouldn't call in a behaviour therapist. Sometimes people who are in an escalated state don't even realize how they're behaving, or the effect their behaviour is having on those around them. Or the person might have insights into what's causing him to behave the way he is, or ideas about what might help to alleviate his distress, if we just take the time to ask, and listen. Listen with an open mind, without judgment. Be curious. Be present. Listen to the person's words, but also listen to his body language, pay attention to non-verbal cues like facial expressions and posture. Sit down next to the person. Slow down. Our temptation might be to speed up and stay one step ahead of the next outburst, but that might actually make the person feel more anxious, and trigger an escalation. Sometimes the best course of action is no action.

Focus on the positive

It's hard to focus on the positive when people come to us in distress or are presented to us in very negative terms. Consider these two different descriptions of Neil:

Description #1: "Neil has many attention-seeking behaviours, like interrupting conversations, pushing ahead of other people, etc. He is very demanding and can become aggressive if he does not get his own way. He knows how to manipulate others to get what he wants, so staff must be firm and consistent in their approach. If Neil senses that he has the upper hand, he will become non-compliant and argumentative with staff."

Description #2: "Neil enjoys being around other people. He has an outgoing personality and he loves a good joke. He likes to take the lead in planning his activities, which staff can support by building in frequent choice-points throughout the day. Neil likes to keep busy and enjoys plenty of physical activity. He prefers the company of people with great social skills and high energy."

If you were Neil, which description would you prefer?

If you were meeting Neil for the first time, what kind of impression would you form about him from these two different descriptions?

Our colleagues Norman Kunc and Emma Van der Klift talk about the importance of one's *narrative*, of the way people talk about themselves and how they are known by others. Often people come to us with a narrative that's been written by someone else – a social worker or service provider – that emphasizes their negative attributes and labels. Each of us has the right to author our own narrative, and most of us wouldn't choose to share the kinds of information that typically gets shared about people when they come into the human service system. We wouldn't introduce ourselves to someone new by saying, *"Hi, I'm Joan and I have high blood pressure,"* or *"I get anxious in new situations,"* but we say things like this about people with developmental disabilities all the time. We introduce people by their labels (*"This is John, he has autism"*) instead of emphasizing their positive qualities. Remember, negative assumptions can become self-fulfilling prophesies. If John has a reputation as a trouble-maker, if that's the way other people view him and that's the most prominent aspect of his narrative, then any time he raises his voice or causes even a minor disturbance we'll see this as validating his reputation. We'll look for trouble-making behaviour because that's the lens we look through when we're with John, and what's worse, he'll come to view himself through this lens. But if instead John's narrative focuses on his love of baseball, or his helpful nature, or some other positive attributes, then that's the lens we'll start to look through when we think of John.

Take a break

My son's grade one teacher used to get her students to do "fence runs" once or twice a day, which involved her opening the classroom door and sending the whole class out to run to the fence on the far side of the field and back again as fast as they could. She did this when things started to get a little escalated in the classroom, and it worked like a charm. The kids loved it, and it was an effective way to defuse the energy in the room. Basically she was recognizing that they needed a break, and she provided them with one before things got out of control, before they even thought to ask for it. Offering someone a break might be a welcome suggestion when things are starting to get a little tense: go for a walk, get a cup of coffee, or just get up and stretch. It can also be a way for people to save face and get out of a situation where they feel backed into a corner. *"Do you want to get a cup of coffee?"* is more respectful, and likely to be more effective, than *"You need to calm down."*

Give the person a role / something to do

If we know that Carl's behaviour tends to escalate in the late afternoon as dinner is approaching, one way to deal with it would be to give him a role. He could make the salad, or set the table for dinner, or choose a cd to play during dinner. Having a role focuses the person's attention on something productive, rather than just waiting for something to happen. It also provides opportunities for natural reinforcement – people will compliment him on the salad, or thank him for setting the table, or talk to him about the music he selected.

Change the environment, not the person

A good assessment and baseline of the behaviour should indicate the conditions or circumstances under which the behaviour is more likely to occur, for example the setting, time of day, other people involved, and so on. Changing one or more of these variables could go far in alleviating the person's distress. If waiting until 6:00 for dinner is just too stressful for Carl, then maybe we could change the schedule and have dinner at 5:00 instead.

Another consideration would be to find environments where the so-called problematic behaviour isn't considered to be problematic. For example, our friend Reggie is greatly amused by bodily functions. He especially used to enjoy loud belching. His staff had the idea of taking Reggie to a downscale (as in, opposite of upscale) sports bar where belching was not considered to be inappropriate, and where Reggie discovered there were other young men who were equally amused by this behaviour. He enjoyed visiting this bar from time to time, but eventually the novelty started to wear off and the belching, too, began to lose its charm for him.

In another example, my friend Brian used to have trouble controlling his temper and would sometimes act out aggressively toward others. We started building in daily outings to the river, where Brian would pick up big rocks and throw them into the water with all his might, until he got tired. The strength required to lift and throw big rocks allowed him to exert all the force he could muster, without hurting himself or anyone else. He got it out of his system, so to speak.

Celebrate successes

One of our managers had this idea for celebrating a person's positive behaviour. Curtis is a young man who sometimes acts out aggressively toward others. He has a file full of critical incident reports (CIRs) going back several years, and every time he has an outburst a new CIR gets filled out and sent to the social worker. The program manager's idea was to start writing PIRs – *positive* incident reports – to document instances when Curtis used other means of getting his needs met instead of resorting to aggression. When he noticed Curtis doing something right, they'd fill out a PIR together. Curtis loved it. He started paying closer attention to his behaviour, and prompting his staff to fill out PIRs as a way of documenting his successes.

It's often the case that people with developmental disabilities are used to getting more negative feedback than positive, in the form of criticism, correction, and if they are seen as having challenging behaviour any number of interventions focused on the so-called problem behaviour. It's important that we recognize and attend to the things people do well, to their strengths, and not just their limitations or weaknesses. People need to hear what they're doing right. They need to be acknowledged for a job well done, and not just corrected when they do something wrong.

Affirmations can be helpful for getting people to focus more on the positive and less on the negative. Affirmations are positive statements about oneself, like *"I make friends easily,"* or *"I am happy and healthy"* – statements that affirm one's self-worth. Repeating affirmative statements, or writing them down and placing them where you'll see them often (on the fridge, on the bathroom mirror) can help to replace the negative self-talk many people carry around with them. So instead of people thinking to themselves, *"I'm not smart enough,"* or *"No-one would want to be my friend,"* they can get in the habit of making positive statements that emphasize their strengths and gifts.

Stress management

We all know the importance of managing stress in our lives. Being able to recognize the signs of stress and manage stress is just as important for someone with a developmental disability as it is for anyone else. Book stores and the local library have whole sections devoted to the topic of stress management, so I won't go into great detail here, but by way of example, some common stress management techniques are:

- Avoid or minimize the source of stress

- Exercise / physical exertion

- Meditation / yoga / guided imagery

- Progressive muscle relaxation

- Deep breathing

- Indulge the senses – listen to music, have a warm bath, light scented candles

- Humour

- Creative expression – make art, dance, sing

- Create a calming physical space – low lighting, comfortable seating, plants, colour

- Spend time in nature

- Stress balls / toys

- Massage

Most of us have multiple ways of dealing with stress. We have things we do proactively, to keep the bad stress at bay (jogging, gardening, having a warm bath before bed, etc.) and we have strategies we can summon when we feel ourselves becoming stressed (go for a walk, make a cup of tea, deep breathing exercises). For someone with a developmental disability – or for anyone, actually – it can be helpful to write down a few preferred strategies and keep them on hand to refer to when necessary. The last thing we need when we're feeling stressed is someone telling us to relax or offering unsolicited advice. It can be more helpful to refer the person to a list of strategies he's pre-selected for himself (as in, *"Gerry, do you have your list handy?"*). Gerry could carry a cue card in his wallet listing his personalized four-step stress management plan, for example:

Gerry's stress management plan

1. *Have a glass of water*

2. *Sit in a comfortable chair*

3. *Take slow, deep breaths for five minutes*

4. *Stand up and stretch*

Stress management is something everyone can benefit from. It relies on an internal locus of control, where behaviour management is externally driven. Positing the person's need for behavioural support as stress management instead of behaviour management is more respectful and more socially valued: many of us have stress management strategies, and we talk openly with others about how we manage our stress, but few of us would accept having behaviour management strategies imposed on us.

We've all seen those studies that calculate the value of a mother's work, as in, *"housekeeping $200/week, professional driver $100/week, cook $250/week, nursing services $100/week,"* and so on. It always adds up to a sizeable sum, the point being that a mother's work is worth as much as that of a doctor or lawyer or CEO, and that it should be valued as much by society. The other point, albeit tongue-in-cheek, is that to replace a mother's work (or father's, to be fair) with paid employees would cost a small fortune. Of course, the value of the relationship is immeasurable, and cannot be replaced. The love and commitment that parents give freely and abundantly to their children cannot be calculated in monetary terms, because the relationship isn't based on economic exchange.

The saying "the best things in life are free" applies to the relationships most of us hold near and dear. The relationships that matter most to us are voluntary, and yet we rely on these relationships for many things. When I needed help moving between apartments back in my university days, I enlisted my friends to help me. When my children were young we sometimes exchanged child care duties with other young families we knew. Occasionally when my car is in the shop I'll get a ride in to the office with a co-worker, and when his car is out of commission I return the favour. The friends who helped me move were paid in pizza and beer – a bargain for me, compared to what it would have cost to pay professional movers, but no-one did the math or asked to be paid for their services. Even people we don't have a close relationship with are generally happy to help out when they can. A while ago, my neighbours hired someone to cut back some overgrown branches on a large tree in their front yard, and offered to prune some of the branches in my yard while they were at it. It was an incremental addition to the work they were already paying for, but it saved me the cost of having to hire someone myself.

We've all had the experience of helping push a stuck car out of the snow. It costs us nothing, but the value to the person stranded in that car is huge. Or the friend of a friend is going camping and needs a tent, so we lend them ours – even if we don't know them personally. Like the value of a mother's work, the value of what we give to each other as friends, neighbours and fellow community members is incalculable.

The scope of a support worker's responsibility might encompass everything from housekeeping to family support to job coaching to fundraising to public relations. Especially in some of our more traditional services, the role of staff sometimes becomes a catch-all comprised of a one part companion, one part teacher, one part nurse, one part housekeeper, etc. But unlike the voluntary role of parent or friend or neighbour, these roles are paid. One response in human services to the multitude of expectations placed on front line supporters has been an increasing specialization of roles, the carving off of different aspects of the person's life or different support functions, into different job categories. There are literally dozens of different titles and job descriptions for those in support positions, each one focused on different dimensions of the relationship between the supporter and the person being supported. It seems everywhere we go we discover another variation. Among the job titles we're aware of are:

- Community support worker
- Life-skills worker
- Residential support worker
- Vocational support worker
- Activity aide
- Behaviour interventionist
- Disability support worker
- Instructor
- Facilitator
- Volunteer
- Paid roommate

- Intervener
- Personal care attendant
- Caregiver
- Rehabilitation worker
- Direct support professional
- Homemaker
- Shared living provider
- Job coach
- Human service worker
- Advocate
- Overnight support worker

Each of these job titles reflects assumptions about role of the person providing the support, and the role of the person being supported. If you're a behaviour interventionist, you will see the person through the lens of his behaviour – so the person's role, then, is to exhibit behaviour for you to intervene with. If you're an activity aide, the person's role is to participate in activities that require your assistance. If you're a caregiver, the person's role is to be the recipient of your care, and so on. This kind of specialization of roles runs the risk of further entrenching people in devalued roles, instead of promoting positive roles. It also presumes a specialist response to people's needs as a first response, rather than looking to more normative responses first. If Kyla wants to expand her repertoire of recreational activities, we could enlist the recreation director at the local community centre to introduce her to some of the activities there, or she could join a gym and work with a trainer to develop a personal workout routine. She might not need an activity aide or community support worker to perform these functions.

Lately we've been using the word "supporter" as a generic term for anyone in a support position. Many of the self advocates we know have told us they prefer this term over "staff," and they prefer it over more specialized language, which many find stigmatizing.

A framework for support

Regardless of the titles we settle on, one thing seems clear: the role of those in direct support positions has changed significantly over the past few decades. When I started in this field back in the 1980s, the support worker role was fairly uniform and straight-forward. Individuals were grouped according to their level of functioning, and were presumed to need 24-hour care. Consistency was key. Support workers were meant to be more or less interchangeable. There were prescribed protocols for personal care routines and household tasks that applied to everyone. I remember the first group home I worked in, there were clipboards hanging on the walls, and attached to the clipboards were task analyses for assorted routines that the residents were expected to complete. A clipboard outside the bathroom held the task analysis for showering, which we used for tracking the showering routine of each of the five residents. One by one, every evening, each person would take his turn having a shower. The staff on duty would follow the person into the bathroom, clipboard in hand, and observe the entire routine, making sure the person completed all of the steps as listed on the task analysis. If someone needed prompting for some of the steps, the staff would document the level of prompt provided on the task analysis – *P* for physical prompt, *V* for verbal prompt, or *G* for gestural prompt. This way, whoever was on duty the next day would know exactly what steps the person was able to do the previous time, and would not over or under-prompt the person during his next shower. Similar checklists were on hand for teeth-brushing, bed-making, laundry, etc. No-one gave much thought to offering people a choice over who assisted them with these routines, or whether they might like to personalize their routines instead of doing exactly the same things in the same way as everyone else. It seems so absurd when I think back on it now, but at the time it was accepted as best practice, in keeping with the logic of the developmental approach.

Today, the individuals and families we meet are coming from a very different context. Most do not require or even want 24-hour care. They might need support for certain kinds of activities, or for certain periods of time, but not necessarily with everything they do, or for all time. Many aspire to a level of independence that would have been considered unrealistic in years past. Increasingly, we're working with people to mobilize a range of supports – formal and informal, paid and unpaid – and helping them build personal routines that reflect their unique lifestyle, rather than merely taking care of people or training them to complete a repertoire of pre-defined tasks. Even people we've been supporting for years are asking for a different kind of support, for more flexibility in how their services are provided. More and more, we're moving away from the idea of prescribed approaches and service models to thinking in terms of personalized support arrangements:

- **Sheila** lives in her own apartment, where she shares access to overnight support with a number of other tenants who live in the same high-rise complex. During the day and evening, she is supported by staff of her choosing. Sheila has a rich network of family, friends and neighbours who she enjoys spending time with, and a microboard that helps her plan her life and direct her supports. She has recently been learning to use an i-pad, which has increased her ability to communicate more freely with people outside of her immediate circle of support. Sheila needs assistance with most of the tasks of daily living, but she's very much in charge of who provides that assistance and directing her supporters to do what she wants to do, in the way she wants things done.

- **Ron** lived in an institution for twenty years before moving into a home that he shares with another man with a developmental disability. Ron gets along well with most people, but he has definite preferences for who provides his support. Prospective staff always come for a meet & greet before being hired into a position, to be sure they're a good match. Ron communicates with some gestures, and he will indicate his choices by positioning himself next to people he wants to spend time with, or helping himself to things he wants, like food, or a bath. Over the years, Ron has re-connected with his family, who live in a small rural community outside of Vancouver. What started as occasional visits with his sister has blossomed into Ron being included in gatherings with his large extended family, and even the occasional overnight visit in their homes. Where Ron's support staff used to take the lead in planning get-togethers and assisting Ron to participate in family functions, over the years his siblings have taken on more of a leadership role in organizing and facilitating these visits.

- **Peter** lived in a variety of situations before coming to our organization for support about 15 years ago. Initially he shared a home with another man with a disability, but they went their separate ways after a couple of years, and Peter tried living with someone else. That didn't last long either, and eventually Peter moved into his own place. He now shares his own home with a university student who receives room and board in exchange for being available to Peter overnight if he needs anything. Peter has a pool of hours available to him for support through the week, and access to several people he's recruited who are available to come in for periods of time to help with things he wants help with. One key support person helps Peter plan his week and organize his supports. He prefers this arrangement to the way it used to be, when the staff schedule was decided for him.

Traditional job descriptions assume a kind of one-size-fits-all approach to community support. But as Sheila, Ron, Peter and others are showing us, the supporter role can play out very differently from one person to the next. In our organization, we've rewritten job descriptions many times in an effort to encompass the wide variety of possible support arrangements. As people move toward greater self determination and self direction, the exceptions start to outnumber the usual way of doing things – the exception to the rule becomes the rule.

Job descriptions are a necessary human resource function in any organization. A good job description articulates the employer's expectations, so employees know what's expected of them, the scope of their duties and responsibilities, etc. But the particulars of the supporter role might change over time, for example if you're supporting someone who has progressed from being quite dependent to being more empowered to direct some aspects of his life. If we look at the role of supporter strictly in terms of a fixed job description, we might be missing the forest for the trees. It might be possible to complete all of the tasks listed in the job description, but still not be helping to advance the person's vision of a good life, and maybe even holding them back. A job description is only as useful as the context within which it's carried out. The context in traditional services is most often a hierarchical structure grounded in systems and processes, but in a person-centred service the context becomes one of partnership. In a hierarchy, the relationships between the various players are fixed, and authority flows from the top down. The expectations and responsibilities of each person in the hierarchy might not change very much over time, and even if change is warranted it's often met with resistance (*"that's not how we do things here," "that's not in my job description"*). In a partnership, relationships are more fluid, and authority is shared more equitably among the various parties. Change is ongoing and to be expected as the partnership evolves. Each person in a partnership is accountable to himself and to the other partners. There's an expectation of continuous learning and improvement that all parties contribute to, and benefit from. A framework for thinking about the support worker role within this context of partnership could be conceptualized as a kind of continuous loop, rather than a linear relationship:

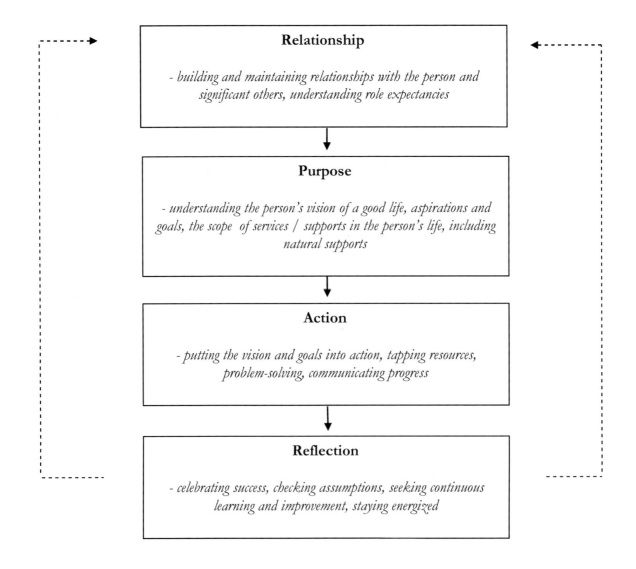

The four parts of this framework represent different aspects of the support worker role that relate to the various topics I've covered thus far. To recap, what follows is a summary of these four broad elements of support:

1.   *Relationship:*

The support worker role starts and ends with the relationship between the supporter and the person(s) being supported. Support worker jobs are not interchangeable. Being guided by the principles of person-centredness and self-determination means we must take great care to match people with supporters based on the criteria that are most important to them, rather than a pre-determined or standardized set of criteria. Before we presume to step into someone's life and start providing them with support, we need to establish a foundation of mutual respect and trust, and this starts with getting the right match and getting to know each other as individuals. Supporters need to spend time with the person, get to know the person's story, where they've come from and where they see their lives heading. We need to know who else is in the person's life – their family, friends, significant others – and how those relationships are interwoven in the person's life. What roles does the person have within their various relationships, at home, in the community, at work? What efforts are being made to deepen and expand the person's network?

Relationships and communication go hand in hand. Does the person have a reliable communication system? How does the person express her wants and needs, and who helps her make important decisions?

Like any relationship, the relationships between supporters and the person / the person's family, friends and significant others will have their ups and downs. Conflict is a natural part of any relationship, and so it's important to talk about how conflicts will get handled, and to resolve conflicts in a positive and constructive way. Unresolved conflict, or factions among the team, can destroy relationships. Think about how you will foster a spirit of teamwork, cooperation and open communication in your day-to-day work.

Think, too, about the assumptions you bring to this work. Looking back at the chart of different positive and negative attitudes, which of these resonates most for you? Some of us grew up at a time when people with disabilities weren't visible in our communities, and we might have had negative assumptions or misconceptions that we've since rethought. Are there assumptions you might be holding onto that could limit your expectations of the person you're supporting now?

2.   *Purpose:*

Over and over again, people tell us that the most important thing supporters can do is listen. Understand what's important to the person by listening to what they have to say. Everyone has hopes and dreams for their future – getting a job, making friends, creating a home of their own – but if someone hasn't been encouraged to dream or provided with opportunities to see what the world has to offer, they might have a very limited vision of what's possible. As people become aware of new possibilities and gain new experiences, their vision starts to expand. They dream bigger. If we're not careful, the needs of the system, and our own assumptions about the person's capacity or how we think supports *should* get organized can start to steer things in a different direction. The person's vision can actually be diminished. Ongoing, thoughtful person-centred planning helps keep the vision alive, and keeps people moving in a positive direction. What is the person's preferred approach to planning, and how does this work? How do supporters contribute to planning? Who organizes and facilitates planning, and who protects the person's plan from other competing interests?

Being attuned to the purpose of support requires a solid understanding of the person's needs. Sometimes we pay more attention to the person's physical and material needs, and less attention to higher order needs like relationships or spirituality. Do you have a good sense of the person's needs in all of the domains we've talked about? Has the person himself had opportunities to talk about and explore each of these areas? Has he had abundant life experiences and opportunities from which to draw, such that he can make informed choices and set ambitious goals? What efforts are being made to broaden the person's range of experiences?

Understanding the person's needs should lead to a better understanding of the vulnerabilities that we need to pay attention to, and will hopefully highlight safeguards that might need to be put in place. Are there factors in the person's life that put him at risk, and if so what efforts are being made to minimize the risks? What supports are in place, both formally and informally, to safeguard the person and minimize potential barriers to a good life in community?

3.   *Action:*

We talked about the importance of putting our time and energy into the things that matter most to the person, the things that will have the greatest impact on her overall quality of life. Think about what you do each day with the person. Is your time together well spent? What is the person's daily / weekly schedule, and does it reflect her stated goals and priorities?

As you spend time together with the person, think about ways that you might start to fade your direct support and promote the person's independence by building her competencies. Are there things the person would like to learn how to do more independently? What is the person's preferred learning style, and what kind of instructional strategies might be most effective? Think about other people you might enlist to help teach a new skill or introduce the person to a new activity. Remember, staff aren't going to be experts at everything people might want to learn. We want to encourage connection with others and take advantage of natural supports wherever possible.

Most of the time that support workers spend with people will be spent in this part of the framework – the action part. It's easy to get caught up in the activities and to-do's of the job, and lose sight of what it is we're working towards, or lose sight of other people who might have a stake in the person's life. Maintaining the lines of communication between all parties is critical. Support workers often spend more time with the person than anyone else, and so they might be the first to notice changes in the person's disposition, behaviour, health, energy level, etc. It's important to be proactively communicating any concerns, and seeking out assistance or a second opinion if you're unsure about anything. Or you might discover as you begin to implement an activity or goal that unforeseen issues come up, or the person changes his mind and wants to focus on something else instead. Again, it's important that others who are involved in the person's life be kept apprised of any changes, and have the opportunity to contribute to discussions and problem-solving around possible next steps.

4.   *Reflection:*

Just as we are constantly reflecting on the person's goals and priorities, it's also important to spend some time reflecting on our own work. How do you define and celebrate success in your work? Do you have access to the support you need to carry out the various aspects of your job? How do you stay energized and inspired?

In traditional services, where groups of staff worked together, there were frequent opportunities to exchange ideas and support each other. In smaller settings and more individualized arrangements, supporters are often working much more independently and might not have as many opportunities to talk to co-workers. You might have more contact with the person's family and friends than you do with your fellow support workers or your supervisor. Having a buddy or mentor is one way to overcome the potential isolation that a supporter might feel, someone to meet with over coffee from time to time. Or be a mentor to someone yourself. Share your learning by helping to train new support workers, writing a newsletter article, or offering to do a presentation to another team. And tell others about your successes – we always love hearing what people are up to, the contributions they're making and connections they're building. Stories of individual lives being well lived are always a joy to hear and provide much hope and inspiration to others. We can never hear too many great stories!

Staff training opportunities, conferences and workshops are a great way to connect with others who are doing similar work, and can also be very energizing. As well, there are many online newsletters, blogs and discussion forums where supporters can connect with like minded people and stay informed about new developments in our field, both locally and abroad. Check out www.101friends.ca as one example!

As we walk with people into their future, new possibilities will arise that we might not even be able to imagine in the present moment. New relationships will emerge, new roles and opportunities will present themselves. Taking a reflective approach to our work will make us more open to seeing possibilities where others might see problems.

The role of supporter is a unique arrangement. It's not a role that other people easily recognize or relate to. Most community members don't have support workers accompanying them through their day. Sometimes people will look at us with puzzled expressions as they try to figure out what exactly it is we're doing. They might be used to seeing staff with groups of people with developmental disabilities going for coffee or going bowling, but not so used to seeing one person with a disability paying for his own coffee at the counter while a support worker sits off to the side. It might not occur to onlookers that the supporter is facilitating the person's independence. The clearer we can be within ourselves about our role in the person's life, the better equipped we'll be to respond when questions come up and ensure that both the person and the supporter are seen in the best possible light.

The framework I've described is grounded in a person-centred approach, in contrast to the program-centred or system-centred approach of traditional services. By way of comparison, I'd like to end with a story that illustrates the importance of having a clear framework for support.

If you build it, they will come: the story of our accidental day program

For our first 15 years, Spectrum steadfastly resisted pressures to open a congregate day program. About ten years ago, we decided to dedicate a small portion of our office as a drop-in space, so that small groups of people could meet, share a few hours of support, and take part in activities of their choosing with others who shared a common interest. The idea came from the individuals and families we were supporting at the time, and was one part of an overall plan to sustain the organization through a period of government restructuring initiatives that resulted in many smaller organizations going out of business. Somewhat reluctantly, we set aside a room in our office, big enough to fit a table and chairs, some shelving for assorted books, games, art supplies and whatnot, but not so big or inviting that it would entice people to want to spend their whole day there. We were very intentional about how we set things up and about communicating our intentions in the most transparent way. Our little drop-in space would allow between six and eight people a day who had few or no dedicated hours of support to access a wider range of opportunities than they'd be able to do on their own. They would be supported by two staff working a combination of hours that would allow for maximum flexibility and individualization, and volunteers would be recruited who shared an interest in whatever activities people might want to pursue – so for example, a college student who was studying recreation used to meet up with a small group once a week to play basketball.

If you build it, they will come

Within a year, the drop-in idea had morphed into something altogether different. Our funders, delighted that we'd finally opened a centre, started referring more "participants" to us. The informality we'd envisioned was soon replaced by a schedule of activities with pre-set start and end times, so instead of people dropping in when they felt like it, they were now being expected to arrive at specific times. Before long, we had between 15 and 20 people coming to our office every day. A sofa appeared in the room one day, presumably a donation. One fellow took to having naps on it in the afternoon, reminiscent of our friend John at the sheltered workshop years before. Then a big screen t.v. and VCR appeared, and people started bringing in videos. *"Just for rainy days,"* it started out, but before long movie afternoons were a recurring activity. Fridays became karaoke day, with people sitting on the floor in a circle singing along to children's songs and playing percussion instruments that someone brought in. A local craft supply store that was going out of business donated their $12,000 worth of inventory – enough to keep everyone busy with arts and crafts for many years to come. This, in turn, created a need for more storage space, so a call went out for a donation of a storage cabinet, which arrived a short time later.

Despite our best efforts to keep things small, flexible and person-centred, our little drop-in space turned into a day program. Rules crept in. People who chose not to participate in the activities that staff organized were being referred to as non-compliant. A spare office down the hall started being used as a "quiet room" for those who needed a break from the noise and constant activity. We arrived one day to find the staff installing lockers out in the hallway, for people to store their coats and backpacks, like one would find in a school. We discovered that a couple of the staff had started fundraising for a passenger van, so they could take bigger groups of people on outings. People started asking for a bigger room. The original rationale for the drop-in space was long forgotten. The new rationale being used to justify the program was that the participants liked being together and needed a separate space to call their own, even though most had had no connection to each other prior to joining the program, and were for all intents and purposes brought together at random.

It became clear to us that our experimental drop-in centre had run its course. And so, we began a process of downsizing the program and moving people back into the community. Over the course of about 18 months, we worked with each individual to come up with community-based alternatives to the group day program, and today all of the participants are pursuing their own interests, which are as varied as the people themselves:

- Kim started volunteering at the local Neighbourhood House, and is now part of the volunteer kitchen crew that prepares and serves hot lunches to area seniors;

- Philip got a job at a coffee shop, where he works independently several days a week. His support hours were moved to the evenings and weekends to focus on helping him expand his social network;
- Rick enjoys visiting the main library downtown, where he works on the computer and has come to know many of the library staff;
- Three of the people who enjoyed making art now take part in a community art class;
- Shane, who used to arrive at our office every day in a wheelchair and spent much of his time sleeping or passively participating in activities, is now walking daily and actively engaged in various community activities;
- Vicky moved to a small seaside community outside of Vancouver, where she enjoys visiting with friends and neighbours and spending time at her local library.

It was amazing to us to see how a number of individuals with unique characteristics and needs could come to be seen as a homogeneous group, in such a short space of time, simply by virtue of being congregated together in one place. Program needs, and the perceived needs of the system for uniformity and control, came to overshadow individual needs. There was a focus on compliance and schedules that didn't exist in our other, more individualized services. The language took on a decidedly more hierarchical flavor. It confirmed for us all the reasons why we'd avoided having such a program for so many years. Seeing these same people now, pursuing activities and lifestyles we couldn't have foreseen a couple of years ago, confirms for us once again that the path to a good life lies in community, not in separate spaces.

I've talked a few times about how our agency is shifting the way we provide services to a more person-centred approach, moving away from the idea of traditional services and focusing more on building strong partnerships with individuals and their networks. Traditional approaches to service delivery tend to view people with developmental disabilities as clients and service recipients, rather than citizens in community. Reflecting back on Wolfensberger's criticism of the "better institution" idea, I can't help but see parallels with some of the issues facing our field today. Regulations and compliance requirements that seem geared toward the creation of ever better programs and services echo the calls for better institutions 40 years ago. Better programs are fine if they lead to better lives for the people who are served by those programs. But if they merely lead to more bureaucracy and standardization, at a time when people are telling us they want less bureaucracy and more flexibility, then we have a problem.

The service system has been very successful at helping people to be physically present in community, but less so at helping them to develop reciprocal relationships and be meaningfully engaged in community. The realization of true community living continues to elude many people with developmental disabilities. We believe that the time is ripe for a new way of working in partnership with individuals and their allies, for taking that final step from the periphery of community life into the thick of it. We know how to do this. We know many people who have defied everyone's predictions of failure and gone on to build enviable lives. Twenty-five years ago the idea of people with severe disabilities being included in community was all a bit experimental, but those days are behind us. When people first started moving out of institutions, there was much fear and uncertainty, many barriers to overcome, but times have changed. The long standing assumption that people with developmental disabilities are safest if they are surrounded by professionals and sheltered in protective environments is giving way to the realization that the most important safeguards are found in community, and in relationship with fellow citizens and community members. To paraphrase David Pitonyak, programs and systems don't keep people safe, relationships keep people safe.

Community living is no longer an idealistic proposition, it's an attainable goal, one that each person deserves the opportunity to realize.

People coming together to share their gifts. Who wouldn't want to be a part of that?

References

Bach, M. & Kerzner, L. (2010). A New Paradigm for Protecting Autonomy and the Right to Legal Capacity. Prepared for the Law Commission of Ontario.

Bank-Mikkelsen, N. (1969). A Metropolitan Area in Denmark: Copenhagen. In Kugel, R. & Wolfensberger, W., eds. *Changing patterns in residential services for the mentally retarded.* Chapter 10, 227-254. Washington, D.C.: President's Committee on Mental Retardation Monograph.

Barnes, C. (1992). Disabling Imagery and the Media: An exploration of the principles of media representations of disabled people. Ryburn Publishing Limited: Halifax, England.

BCACL (2010). A Guide to Celebrating Canada's Ratification of the UN Convention on the Rights of Persons with Disabilities.

Blatt, B. (1969). Purgatory. In Kugel, R. & Wolfensberger, W., eds. *Changing patterns in residential services for the mentally retarded.* Chapter 3, 36-49. Washington, D.C.: President's Committee on Mental Retardation Monograph.

Brown, L., Nietupski, J. & Hamre Nietupski, S. (1976). The Criterion of Ultimate Functioning and Public School Services for Severely Handicapped Students. *Hey, Don't Forget about Me: Education's investment in the severely, profoundly and multiply handicapped, (2-15).* Reston, Virginia: Council for Exceptional Children.

Bunch, G., Finnegan, K. & Pearpoint, J. (2009). *Planning for Real Life After School: Ways for families and teachers to plan for students experiencing significant challenge.* Toronto: Inclusion Press.

CACL (2011). Achieving Social and Economic Inclusion: From segregation to employment first. Toronto, Ontario.

CLBC (2009). Addressing Personal Vulnerability Through Planning: A guide to identifying and incorporating intentional safeguards when planning with adults with developmental disabilities and their families.

Callahan, M. (2007). Embracing a Working Life for All. *TASH Connections,* January/February 2007: 16-18.

Carter-Hollingsworth, J. & Apel, L. (2008). The 7 Wonders of the World of Disabilities. *Exceptional Parent*, November 2008: 50-55.

Charlton, James. (1998). *Nothing About Us Without Us: Disability oppression and empowerment.* University of California Press.

Cocks, E. (2001). Normalization and Social Role Valorization: Guidance for human service development. *Hong Kong Journal of Psychiatry, 2001, 11(1):* 12-16.

Collier, N. (1995). *History,* BCACL website. Internet URL: http://www.bcacl.org/about-us/history

DeJong, G. (1979). Independent Living: from social movement to analytic paradigm. *Archives of Physical Medicine and Rehabilitation, 60,* October 1979: 435-446.

Driedger, D. (1989). *The Last Civil Rights Movement: Disabled people's international.* New York: St. Martin's Press.

DSM-IV (1994). Criteria for Posttraumatic Stress Disorder. Quoted on Mental Health Today website: http://www.mental-health-today.com/ptsd/dsm.htm

Dybwad, G. (1969). Action Implications, U.S.A. Today. In Kugel, R. & Wolfensberger, W., eds. *Changing patterns in residential services for the mentally retarded.* Chapter 17, 383-426. Washington, D.C.: President's Committee on Mental Retardation Monograph.

Ericsson, K. (1985). The Principle of Normalization: History and experiences in Scandinavian countries. Presentation, ILSMH Congress. Hamburg, 1985.

Falvey, M., Forest, M., Pearpoint, J. & Rosenberg, R. (2000). *All My Life's a Circle: Using the tools: circles, MAPs & PATHs.* Toronto: Inclusion Press.

Ferster, C. and Skinner, B. (1957). Schedules of Reinforcement. Appleton-Century-Crofts, New York.

Gladwell, M. (2005). *Blink: The power of thinking without thinking.* New York: Time Warner Book Group. Chapter 3, 72-98.

Gold, M. (1980). *"Did I Say That?" Articles and commentary on the Try Another Way system.* Champaign, Illinois: Research Press Company.

Goode, B. (2011). *The Goode Life: Memoires of disability rights activist Barb Goode.* Vancouver: Spectrum Press.

Groce, N. (1985). *Everyone Here Spoke Sign Language: Hereditary deafness on Martha's Vineyard.* Cambridge: Harvard University Press.

Heller, H., Spooner, F., Enright, B., Haney, K., and Schilit, J. (1991). Classic Articles: A Reflection into the Field of Mental Retardation. *Education and Training in Mental Retardation, 26,* 1991: 202-206.

Holt-Lunstad, J., Smith, TB & Layton JB. (2010). Social Relationships and Mortality Risk: A Meta-analytic Review. *PLoS Med 7*(7): e1000316.

Johannes, A., Reynolds, J. & Stanfield, S. (2011). *101 Ways to Facilitate Making Friends: How to engage and deepen support networks for people with disabilities.* Vancouver: Spectrum Press.

Johannes, A. & Stanfield, S. (2011). *101 Ways to Make Friends: Ideas and conversation starters for people with disabilities and their supporters, 2ⁿᵈ edition.* Vancouver: Spectrum Press.

Kendrick, M. (1996). The Natural Authority of Families. *Crucial Times, (6).* Brisbane, Australia.

Kendrick, M. (2009). Personal Fulfillment, Values and the Role of Supportive Communities. *TASH Connections,* Fall 2009: 17-20.

Kendrick, M. (undated). Normative/Universal Needs: Domains of Need. OISD course materials.

Kendrick, M. (2011). Empowerment and Self-Direction Relative to the Design and Governance of Personalized Service Arrangements. *Journal of Human Development, Disability, and Social Change, (19),* 2, 57-68.

Kretzmann, J. & McKnight, J. (1993). *Building Communities from the Inside Out: A path toward finding and mobilizing a community's assets.* Evanston, Illinois: Center for Urban Affairs and Policy Research.

Kunc, N. & Van der Klift, E. (2012). The Person is Not the Problem. The Problem is the Problem! Penticton: BCACL Annual Conference.

Lavigna, G. & Donnellan, A. (1986). *Alternatives to Punishment: Solving behavior problems with non-aversive strategies.* New York: Irvington Publishers.

LaVigna, G. & Willis, T. (1992). Challenging Behavior: A model for breaking the barriers to social and community integration. *Positive Practices, 1*(1), October 1995.

Lord, J. (2001). Self-determination and Community: Building a Textured Life. *The Communicator,* January 2001.

Lord, J. & Hutchison, P. (2007). *Pathways to Inclusion: Building a new story with people and communities.* Concord: Captus Press.

Lord, J., Leavitt, B. & Dingwall, C. (2012). *Facilitating an Everyday Life: Independent facilitation and what really matters in a new story.* Toronto: Inclusion Press.

Lovett, H. (1996). Community is not a Place but a Way of Life. From a speech made in Dallas in 1996, reprinted in *Adult Autism Issues in Waterloo-Wellington,* October 2002.

McKnight, J. (1995). *The Careless Society: community and its counterfeits.* New York: Harper-Collins Publishers, Inc.

Mcloughlin, C., Garner, J. & Callahan, M. (1987). *Getting Employed, Staying Employed: Job development and training for persons with severe handicaps.* Baltimore: Brookes Publishing.

Ministry of Education. (2007). Planning 10: Integrated Resource Package 2007. British Columbia: Ministry of Education.

Mount, B. (2000) *Life Building: Opening windows to change using Personal Futures Planning workbook.* New York: Capacity Works.

NACDD (2011). The Time is Now: Embracing employment first. Washington, DC.

Nerney, Thomas. Communicating Self-Determination: Freedom, Authority, Support and Responsibility. The Centre for Self-Determination website: http://www.centerforself-determination.com/sd.html

Nirje, B. (1969). A Scandinavian Visitor Looks at U.S. Institutions. In Kugel, R. & Wolfensberger, W., eds. *Changing patterns in residential services for the mentally retarded.* Chapter 4, 51-58. Washington, D.C.: President's Committee on Mental Retardation Monograph.

Nirje, B. (1969). The Normalization Principle and its Human Service Implications. In Kugel, R. & Wolfensberger, W., eds. *Changing patterns in residential services for the mentally retarded.* Chapter 7, 179-195. Washington, D.C.: President's Committee on Mental Retardation Monograph.

Matthews, G. (2008). Goals Research Summary. Internet URL http://sidsavara.com/wp-content/uploads/2008/09/researchsummary2.pdf

O'Brien, J. (1989). What's Worth Working For? Leadership for better quality human services. Lithonia, Georgia: Responsive Systems Associates.

O'Brien, J. (1991). Down Stairs that are Never Your Own: Supporting people with developmental disabilities in their own homes. Lithonia, GA: Responsive Systems Associates.

O'Brien, J. & Blessing, C. (2011). *Conversations on Citizenship & Person-Centred Work.* Toronto: Inclusion Press.

O'Brien, J. & Lyle-O'Brien, C. (1988). *A Little Book about Person-Centred Planning.* Toronto: Inclusion Press.

O'Brien, J. & Lyle-O'Brien, C. (1994). Assistance with Integrity: The search for accountability and the lives of people with developmental disabilities. Responsive Systems Associates Inc.

O'Brien, J. & Lyle-O'Brien, C. (2000). The Origins of Person-Centred Planning: A community of practice perspective. Responsive Systems Associates Inc.

OECD Better Life Initiative. Internet URL: http://www.oecdbetterlifeindex.org/

Perske, R. (1988). *Circle of Friends: People with disabilities and their friends enrich the lives of one another.* Nashville: Abingdon Press.

Perske, R. (1981). *Hope for the Families: New directions for parents of persons with retardation or other disabilities.* Nashville: Abingdon Press.

Pitonyak, D. (2006). The Importance of Belonging. *TASH Connections, 32,* January/February 2006.

Razza, N., Tomasulo, D. & Sobsey, D. (2011). Group Psychotherapy for Trauma-Related Disorders in People with Intellectual Disabilities. *Advances in Mental Health and Intellectual Disabilities.* Vol. 5(5), 40-45.

Rowe, M. (1986). Wait Time: Slowing down may be a way of speeding up! *Journal of Teacher Education.* 1986, 37, 43-50.

Sobsey, D. (1994). *Violence and Abuse in the Lives of People with Disabilities: The end of silent acceptance?* Baltimore, MD: Brooks Publishing.

Snow, J. (undated). Creating What I Know About Community. Toronto: Inclusion Press.

Snow, J. (2001). The Quiet Voice. Internet URL http://www.communityworks.info/judithmessage.htm

TASH International (2000). Resolution on the Right to Communicate.

Thomas, S. & Wolfensberger, W. (1969). An Overview of Social Role Valorization. In Flynn, R. & Lemay, R., eds. *A quarter century of normalization and social role valorization: evolution and impact.* Chapter 5, 125-159. Ottawa: University of Ottawa Press.

UN Convention on the Rights of Persons with Disabilities. (2006). Internet URL http://www.un.org/disabilities/convention/conventionfull.shtml

US Department of Labor website. *Customized Employment.* Internet URL http://www.dol.gov/odep/categories/workforce/CustomizedEmployment/what/index.htm

Waddell, G. & Burton, A. (2006). Is Work Good for your Health and Well-Being? London. TSO (The Stationary Office).

Wehman, Paul (2007). *Real Work for Real Pay: Inclusive employment for people with disabilities.* Baltimore: Brookes Publishing.

Willig Levy, Chava (1998). A People's History of the Independent Living Movement. Internet publication URL: www.independentliving.org/docs5/ILhistory.html

Wolfensberger, W. (1969). The Origin and Nature of Our Institutional Models. In Kugel, R. & Wolfensberger, W., eds. *Changing patterns in residential services for the mentally retarded.* Chapter 5, 59-171. Washington, D.C.: President's Committee on Mental Retardation Monograph.

Wolfensberger, W. (1972). *The Principle of Normalization in Human Services.* Toronto: National Institute on Mental Retardation.

Wolfensberger, W. (1983). Social Role Valorization: A proposed new term for the principle of normalization. *Mental Retardation, 21*(6), 234-239.

Wolfensberger, W. (1999). A contribution to the history of Normalization, with primary emphasis on the establishment of Normalization in North America between 1967-1975. In Flynn, R. & Lemay, R., eds. *A quarter century of normalization and social role valorization: evolution and impact.* Chapter 3, 51-116. Ottawa: University of Ottawa Press.

Yates, J. (1999). The North American formulation of the principle of normalization. In Flynn, R. & Lemay, R., eds. *A quarter century of normalization and social role valorization: evolution and impact.* Chapter 4, 117-123. Ottawa: University of Ottawa Press.